DISCOVERY
FINDING THE BURIED TREASURE

Dear George,
Celebrate all your special gifts. Celebrate you.
With love,
Jerry

JERRY MOE

A Prevention/Intervention Program for Youths from High Stress Families

SIERRA TUCSON EDUCATIONAL MATERIALS PUBLICATIONS

The examples presented here are composites of many children. All names, identifying characteristics, and other details have been changed to protect anonymity.

Illustrated by Jane Barton

Published by

STEM Publications
P.O. Box 8307
Tucson, Arizona 85738
(602) 792-5819
(800) 521-7836

ISBN 0-922-641-93-5

DEDICATION

To Michelle, a constant source of love and inspiration in my life. Thanks for believing in me.

ACKNOWLEDGMENTS

This book would never have happened without the love and support of many colleagues, family members, and friends. Special thanks go to William T. O'Donnell, Jr., CEO and chairman of the board, Sierra Tucson, for his unyielding commitment to providing quality services to young children as an integral part of the healing and recovery process. From Bill's leadership on down, through the executive committee, program directors, and all staff members, Sierra Tucson's family systems approach to treating addiction, codependency, and mental health problems includes providing age-appropriate programs for youngsters in an effort to create a new legacy of health and wellness. While many programs only talk about serving the whole family, Sierra Tucson actively includes children as an important part of the equation.

My sincere appreciation goes to Leroy Bishop, Wyatt Webb, Holly McCarter, Gayle Richter, and Michal Gorman. Your love, support, guidance, and enthusiasm have deeply touched and sustained me on this journey.

Theresa Nowotny, with a big assist from Carol Arthur, Doris Bostic and Donna Peterson computerized the text initially and offered valuable suggestions, a gargantuan task in and of itself. Thanks for all of your valuable time and assistance. Kim Payne provided her organizational expertise at a time when I was ready to give up.

Many others gave so willingly and lovingly of themselves to make this a reality. Jim Belanger guided me along with his gentle manner. Karen Chatfield edited the text and made many valuable suggestions. Lynn Bishop, with a big assist from Gael Stirler, provided her graphic design gifts in a loving and caring way. Jane Barton brought the text to life with her wonderful illustrations. Thanks to Daniel Conroy, Wendy Silva, Don Pohlman, and Marilyn Durick for their help. What a gift to have all of you in my life!

Most of all, many thanks to the children I've been blessed to work with over the years. Without you this would only be a dream. Thank you for being my teachers. You have deeply moved and touched my heart in so, so many ways. For this I am eternally grateful.

Contents

Part 1: PROGRAM DEVELOPMENT

Part 2: DAILY ACTIVITIES

FOREWORD

As President of Onsite Training and Consulting, Inc. and Founding Chairperson of the National Association for Children of Alcoholics (NACoA), I have worked with many people in the field of addictions and codependency. One of the more enlightening therapists and teachers that I have been associated with is Jerry Moe. Onsite Training and Consulting has used Jerry's services many times and has had nothing but outstanding feedback. Jerry is a constant source of strength and compassion with incredible talent. When I became the founding chairperson for NACoA my intent was to help inspire more people to do the type of work that Jerry has done.

I would like to congratulate the Sierra Tucson Treatment Center for having the wisdom and foresight to install a specific program for young children of alcoholics. In addition, I would like to thank them for their support of Jerry Moe's book, *Discovery...Finding the Buried Treasure*. Never have I seen such a well written, thought-out book. Jerry explains in detail his work with children in a concise and clear way that any professional can emulate. All of the exercises and tools mentioned in the book can just as easily be understood and followed.

I have worked with children from alcoholic histories for twenty-two years and have watched children grow from adolescents into adulthood with fewer problems and more self-worth because of programs such as the one Jerry describes in this book.

I have long believed in the importance of treating the whole family system, as well as the children deeply affected by the disease of addiction/codependency. The *Discovery* program utilizes several techniques in reuniting family bonds. By emphasizing a strong parental connection as well as involvement by other family members, the program aims to restore communication, trust, and intimacy. I believe that "Family Week," a fundamental part of the program, is one of the most effective means of accomplishing these goals. In an attempt to bring family members closer to one another, through lecture and varied group interaction, "Family Week" addresses the needs of each family member.

I am also quite impressed by the way in which the *Discovery* program works with children, giving careful attention to their age and individuality. It is obvious from the sculptures described in this book that Jerry and Sierra Tucson have worked hard in creating a setting that is conducive to the vastly different needs of the many children who attend this program. The program has activities such as "Feeling Puppet Family," which helps young children who have undeveloped social and verbal skills to adequately express themselves. "Jeopardy — the Self-Care Game," which gives older children the opportunity to learn self-care concepts while learning to cooperate and work together as a team, has proven to be very effective. In the words of Jerry Moe, "The seeds of addiction and codependency are sown in childhood...and it is here

[Sierra Tucson] that the seeds of health and wellness are sown." I strongly believe that this is the essence of the success of this program.

I have recently visited Sierra Tucson and was very touched by the feelings of true love and concern from all involved in this program. These feelings are also conveyed throughout Jerry's book. Through careful administration of the process outlined in the book, the counselors strive to put themselves on the same level as the children. They validate and help empower the children, and most importantly, they LOVE the children.

As Paul Hamly Furfey wrote in *The Church and the Child,* 1933, "The first, the most fundamental right of childhood is the right to be loved. The child comes into the world alone, defenseless, without resource. Only love can stand between infant helplessness and savagery of the harsh world." At Sierra Tucson, the children that attend the *Discovery* program are rediscovering their fundamental right to be loved.

If your goal is to assist children from dysfunctional families, I highly recommend this book about the *Discovery* program and Sierra Tucson, and am extremely supportive of both. This program should serve as a model for treatment centers throughout the country.

Although this is one of the best I've ever read, Jerry and I agree that people should seek additional training, both professional and personal, and should not rely on reading alone. This book, used in cooperation with accepted therapeutic techniques, may greatly enhance the ability to reach more children more effectively.

Sharon Wegscheider-Cruse, *President*
Onsite Training and Consulting, Inc.

Author of *Another Chance: Hope and Health for the Alcoholic Family; The Family Trap; The Miracle of Recovery; Learning to Love Yourself;* and many other publications.

INTRODUCTION

Welcome to *Discovery... Finding the Buried Treasure,* a prevention/intervention program for youth from high stress families. Today there's much hope for children living in stressful family systems, because they can initiate and deepen their own recovery while they are still young. With help they can interrupt the multigenerational cycle of addiction, codependency, and other compulsive behaviors. They can actively participate in creating a new legacy, one of health and wellness. By developing a variety of essential life skills, children may lead full and balanced lives even if stifling problems continue to challenge their families.

Sierra Tucson treats individuals for alcoholism, other addictions, mental health problems, codependency, and trauma resolution using a holistic approach that encompasses body, mind and spirit, intense feelings work, the disease concept of addiction, the Twelve Steps, the integration of family-of-origin issues, and the belief that recovery is a lifelong process. Because addiction and mental health problems can impact the entire family, Sierra Tucson strongly emphasizes the involvement of family members during the patient's stay through their participation in family week. Children deeply experience family problems and stress, yet they typically are forgotten or ignored during treatment. Instead of expecting youngsters to fit into the adult-focused family groups, it is essential that they have an age-appropriate safe place to share feelings, talk openly, come to understand what's been happening at home, and to develop new coping skills.

During the past few years at Sierra Tucson I have developed, implemented, and continually refined a children's program designed to introduce youngsters to their own healing. This model works and can be easily adapted for treatment centers, psychiatric hospitals, outpatient programs, child guidance clinics, and other community-based treatment centers. This program may be used as a family week experience or adapted for youth retreats, summer camps, or even weekly hour-long sessions.

This book is structured for easy access and reference. Chapter 1 provides an overview of Sierra Tucson by exploring its mission statement, shared values and philosophy, and the environment where this program was developed. Chapter 2 explores the goals, daily themes, and suggested format of the children's program. Chapter 3 focuses on an essential program component, the children's facilitators. Effective programs depend on healthy, quality facilitators. Here we discuss typical facilitator tasks and desired qualities. Chapter 4 briefly examines working with parents. By clearly communicating and treating parents with dignity and respect, the groundwork for a positive partnership can be laid. Chapter 5 covers such nuts-and-bolts strategies as planning sessions, group rules, opening and closing exercises, and dealing with suspected abuse.

Chapters 6–10 bring daily themes to life through over fifty-five games and activities. Each game is clearly explained with a description, example, affirmations, materials required, and additional comments. These activities, stressing bonding, trust, cooperation, and teamwork, allow children to be kids. Often in the safety of laughter, play, and bonding, youngsters gain new insight, share painful feelings, and develop new coping skills, all essentials to healing. These games work well with adolescents and adults, too.

While *Discovery . . . Finding the Buried Treasure* has its origins in a treatment center, it can easily be adapted to a variety of other community settings (see *Conducting Support Groups for Elementary Children K-6: A Guide for Educators and Other Professionals,* Johnson Institute, 1991). Churches, recreation programs, juvenile detention facilities, scout programs, shelters, and other community groups can adapt this model to best meet their various needs. However, activities such as tough love lists and forgiveness and reconciliation exercises are only appropriate in the context of family week programs to ensure the children's safety and well-being. Here youngsters and patients participate in an intensive, structured process with highly trained counselors.

Teachers, school psychologists, administrators, nurses, social workers and educational support group facilitators may also find this book very useful and helpful. Many schools have developed excellent prevention programs and student assistance program models that truly make a difference in the lives of children. They will especially benefit from the games and activities featured here; you can simply never have enough tools in your box. The information presented herein can enrich any school's efforts, whether it be the highly developed program boosted by an infusion of new ideas and strategies or a program starting from scratch.

Please don't use this book as your sole guide. Effective facilitators need special training, education, and ongoing support. Take advantage of the rich resources available to assist your efforts. Regional and national trainings, workshops, and conferences provide excellent learning and enrichment opportunities. Books, videos, and audios can be new sources of information, insight, and support. Local colleges and universities sometimes offer courses and seminars relevant to your needs. Most important, focus on your personal recovery, because it is essential to have health to give to kids. You can have a powerful impact on the lives of many youngsters by being a positive role model, someone who takes good care of himself or herself. Walk the talk, let it begin with you.

What a blessing to watch children grow and develop! Playful games and activities help youngsters connect their heads and hearts, take healthy risks, and try out new life skills. As the process unfolds, children get in touch with their intrinsic beauty, goodness, and worth. These qualities had always been inside, yet they somehow got lost amidst the family problems, stress, and chaos. What a joy to watch youngsters find their buried treasure! Please join me on this incredible journey, *Discovery...Finding the Buried Treasure.*

PART 1

Program Development

An Overview of Sierra Tucson

Sierra Tucson Treatment Center—Mission Statement

Sierra Tucson is a publicly held corporation dedicated to the resolution of chemical and non-chemical dependencies. It is based on the Twelve Step concept and committed to the delivery of professional services emphasizing the value and worth of the individual in a loving environment. These dependencies are treated using a systemic family model encompassing mind, body, and spirit. This is achieved through the highest level of care delivered by a staff committed to open communication, teamwork, and the principles of recovery.

Sierra Tucson is committed to growth and development through innovative leadership in a variety of programs consistent with our primary purpose. The organization is dedicated to meeting its community responsibility by developing and utilizing its national and international presence through its commitment to research, education, awareness, prevention, and treatment.

Shared Values

Here is a list of the values we share at Sierra Tucson that address our commitment to patients and staff and the principles that guide us:

THE TWELVE STEPS

RECOVERY
• Provide an environment and programs that promote recovery

RESPECT AND VALUE THE SIERRA TUCSON "FAMILY"
• Commitment to personal and professional growth
• Acknowledge individual contributions
• Maintain a nurturing environment
• Family feelings

QUALITY
- Leading edge/state-of-the-art
- Set the standard

INTEGRITY
- Practice the principles in all of our affairs
- Courage to do what we say

SYSTEMS/FAMILY
- Addiction is a family/system disease
- Recovery is a process
- Healing mind, body, spirit
- Spiritual focus

WORK AS A VALUE, NOT AN ADDICTION
- Balance the interest of the individual with the interest of the organization
- Success is a result of commitment
- Have fun

GROWTH AND DEVELOPMENT
- Willingness to change
- Innovative leadership
- Vision
- Flexibility

OPEN COMMUNICATION
- Encourage the sharing of information
- Ability to learn

TEAMWORK
- Working together to achieve common goals
- Sharing the wins and losses

SHARING THE AWARENESS
- National presence
- "Community" responsibility, carry the message

Family Week

Usually occurring the third week of a patient's treatment, family week at Sierra Tucson aims to restore open communication, trust, and intimacy among family members. Sierra Tucson offers a recovery plan that addresses the needs of each family member. Trained staff, as well as other families affected by addiction and/or mental health concerns, provide support and understanding for the confusion and aching isolation typical of these problems. We believe that anyone who has been affected by addiction or mental health concerns deserves a chance to heal and recover.

Family week focuses on sharing concerns with other family members, gaining knowledge and insight about addiction and mental health issues, and learning more about oneself and one's family.

The morning features a lecture, followed by a small group experience with other families. The small group provides an opportunity for participants to share feelings and concerns with people who can understand. The opportunity also exists to gain helpful information to deepen one's understanding of addiction and mental health concerns. This information will hopefully enable family members to live fuller and richer lives.

After lunch each day a presentation is made on a variety of pertinent recovery topics. Family members also participate in a group with the patient. In patient group, family members can make a new start by honestly and openly sharing their perceptions and feelings in a safe and supportive environment.

Children participate in patient group three times weekly, but they spend the majority of their time in a specially designed children's program. This prevention program introduces six-to-twelve-year-olds to a variety of healthy living skills. Primarily through fun and play, children also get the chance to begin the healing and recovery process.

Sierra Tucson Children's Program

Addiction and codependency are a disease of body, mind, emotion, and soul. In a cunning, powerful, and baffling way, this disease harms all family members who come in its path. Children are particularly impacted by addiction, codependency and mental health problems, as they can consume their parents and other loved ones in ways youngsters simply can't comprehend. The seeds of addiction and codependency are sown in childhood.

Today over seven million American children under the age of eighteen are growing up with at least one alcoholic parent. On average, one out of every five students in any classroom across our country lives with parental alcoholism as a central unifying aspect of his or her life. These children are at high risk for a variety of problems:

- Children of alcoholics have a four-to-five times greater risk of alcoholism and other drug addiction than children of nonalcoholics. Physiological and environmental factors contribute to the risk of becoming addicted.

- Children of alcoholics and other drug-addicted parents exhibit a broad range of symptoms of depression and anxiety.

- Fetal Alcohol Syndrome is one of three known leading causes of mental retardation and is the only one that is entirely preventable.

- Children of alcoholics are more likely to be truant, drop out of school, repeat grades, or be referred to a school counselor or psychologist. This pattern may have little to do with academic performance and more to do with not bonding to teachers and other students, school anxiety related to performance, and fear of failure.
- Children of alcoholics are disproportionately represented in the courts, mental health facilities, hospitals, juvenile justice system, and/or as referrals to school authorities.

Add to this the growing number of children living with parents addicted to drugs other than alcohol. Addiction and codependency become a family legacy that gets passed from generation to generation. Where does it stop?

Other children also know this silence and suffering. In their families addiction to food, sex, relationships, work, gambling, and/or mental health concerns creates a similarly stifling environment of tension, fear, isolation, and pain that puts the children at high risk. Their families may feature severe conflict, neglect, parents as poor role models, disruption of family rituals, frequent moves, and increased risks of verbal, physical, and sexual abuse. Children often express feelings of being unloved or rejected by one or both parents. Their main concern is parental fighting, coupled with the inconsistency and unpredictability found in their homes. Children of addiction often adapt to the chaos and inconsistency at home by developing an inability to trust, express feelings, form close relationships, or value their own worth, all characteristics of codependency and addiction.

These children learn to manipulate as they live with insecurity and fear. Above all, they stop being children, as they carry adult worries, problems, and concerns. Addiction and codependency can rob them of the joy, magic, wonder, and spontaneity of being kids.

Sierra Tucson features a unique prevention and early intervention program for children during family week. The program rests on four basic cornerstones:

- Children deserve the right to their own recovery and healing.
- Children deserve to be treated with the same dignity, respect, value, and worth afforded to adults.
- Children deserve to be listened to and heard.
- Children deserve the opportunity to be kids.

The children's program assists youngsters in the recovery process in a systematic, comprehensive manner. Through understanding the disease of addiction and codependency in an age appropriate way, children come to see that they are not at fault, and that they are not alone. The program emphasizes helping children to identify and express their feelings, to talk openly and freely about what living with these family problems has been like. As they break their silence, children learn new skills to express their feelings in healthy and safe ways. They begin to unload the excess baggage of stifled emotions and problems they've been lugging around. Children are re-vitalized and their hearts become lighter.

The program also teaches youngsters a variety of problem solving, coping, and self-care tools. Children realize they have choices in how they respond to life events and that it's okay to ask for help along the way. Provided with maps that identify safe people, youngsters are empowered to take good care of themselves and to stay safe. Most important, at Sierra Tucson children come to celebrate their intrinsic beauty and worth, as each child is truly one of a kind. Through this process they come to trust and believe in themselves, often for the first time in their lives.

Above all else, the program allows children to be kids, to laugh, play, be curious, and explore. Children of addiction can play their way to health and understanding through art, music, movement, role playing, story telling, and specially designed games, all of which impart positive, healthy living skills. Youngsters can discover their precious child within and experience the joy, magic, and wonder of childhood. It is at these moments that children get reconnected to their hearts. This awakening is at the very core of recovery. It provides an incredible opportunity to break the multigenerational cycle of addiction and codependency, for it is here that health and wellness begin, the genesis of a new family legacy.

CHAPTER 2

An Overview of the Children's Program

Children's Program Goals

The Children's Program helps youngsters to:

1. Explore and express feelings in a safe and supportive environment.

Upon learning that all feelings are okay, children begin to talk freely and express emotions about what's been going on in their families. As more and more feelings surface, children explore how to express them in safe and healthy ways. Group provides the security needed for children to cast aside the "don't talk" and "don't feel" rules.

2. Understand addiction and codependency in an age-appropriate way.

Once children begin to gain knowledge about the disease of addiction and codependency, they may come to fully realize that they are not to blame, and that they are not alone. Youngsters understand why family members act as they do and are then ready to integrate new coping skills to handle things beyond their control.

3. Learn a variety of problem solving, coping, and self-care strategies.

Children learn that they have options in dealing with difficult problems and situations. Often for the first time in their lives, they realize that asking for help is okay. Equipped with maps of safe people, children are empowered with new ways to stay safe and take care of themselves.

4. Build self-esteem, self-worth, and positive feelings about themselves.

Hurt, confusion, fear, guilt, and shame often consume youngsters living in addicted and/or codependent families, as sometimes there is very little to celebrate. At Sierra Tucson, children come to see that they are unique, filled with beauty and special gifts. They begin to feel positive about themselves and to realize they are worthy of respect and love.

5. Trust themselves and others.

The "don't trust" rule, so pervasive in addicted and codependent families, is constantly reinforced by the chaos, inconsistency, unpredictability, and broken promises at home. Children living in this environment begin to distrust others and themselves. In group, youngsters gradually begin to trust their facilitators, a key first step to trusting safe people. They also begin to trust their own perceptions and gut instincts about what makes certain people safe or unsafe.

6. Realize they are not alone.

Children feel incredible relief when they realize that others have had similar feelings and problems with addiction and/or codependency in their homes. This common bond fosters open discussion and sharing of feelings with others who have lived with this pain and craziness. Children learn that they can get support from people who have been through the same experience and really know what it's like.

7. Simply be kids by learning to have fun in safe and healthy ways.

With clear rules, consistently enforced consequences, and healthy group leaders to guide the process, children can let go of the surrogate adult roles they so often assume in their families. Specially designed games, activities, and recreation help children to laugh, play, explore, and just be kids for a little while. Through play, youngsters not only discover and affirm their inner value, but also get reconnected to their hearts in the process.

DAILY THEMES

The following themes are presented and emphasized throughout the week. See chapters 6-10 for an in-depth discussion of daily activities.

MONDAY	**Not My Fault** (Family Addiction and Codependency)
TUESDAY	**All My Feelings Are Okay** (Feelings)
WEDNESDAY	**Taking Care of Me** (Problem Solving and Self-care)
THURSDAY	**I Am Special** (Self-worth)
FRIDAY	**Celebrate Me** (Good-byes and Hellos)

The following paragraphs describe a typical day in the children's program at Sierra Tucson:

DESCRIPTION OF DAILY FORMAT COMPONENTS

1. Opening

Opening exercises attempt to make youngsters feel more comfortable and safe in group. Openers may include introductions, group rules, check-ins, and an open-ended question to get things rolling. These icebreakers set the tone for the group by initiating interaction, building trust, and focusing and balancing the group's energy level.

Many children, nervous and scared about this new experience, are initially reluctant to share thoughts and feelings in group. A simple question like, "Who's your favorite cartoon character?" or "What one thing would you change if you were king or queen of the world for one day?" can help to break the ice and let children see that group can be fun. Openers allow youngsters to participate from the outset, because the longer children wait to speak up, the harder it becomes to do so. Opening exercises also welcome children and assist them in settling into the group process. Begin each day with introductions, group rules, and a fun question. (See section on group openers in chapter 5.)

2. Daily Theme

Each day of the children's program has a specific theme and focus. The day's activities integrate this theme physically, mentally, emotionally, socially, and spiritually. The daily theme is a didactic and experiential process wherein the group facilitator introduces children to the key concepts and relevant information about the topic of the day. This mini-lecture establishes the day's focus and gives basic information related to the topic. Lasting approximately thirty to forty-five minutes, this presentation sets the table for the banquet of insight, healing, and skill development that takes place the rest of the day. Facilitators are encouraged to creatively translate this important information into their own language and a style of delivery that children can easily comprehend.

3. Recreation

Here's an opportunity for children to exercise their bodies and simultaneously contemplate the key information of the daily theme. Activities may include a short hike, a sports activity or an outside game of follow the leader. Hearts pumping and lungs breathing fresh air out in the sun, children enjoy this time together as they integrate the day's theme and focus. They are starting to take better care of their bodies in the process.

4. Creative Activities

Experiential activities reinforce the key concepts of the daily themes and make the information come to life for the children. Such hands-on exercises as art, puppets, role-plays, music, and movement allow youngsters to experience ideas and concepts that touch a variety of senses. These activities provide an opportunity for children to integrate and internalize this important information. A Chinese proverb says it best:

> *When I hear something, I forget it.*
>
> *When I see something, I remember it.*
>
> *When I do something, I understand it.*

Creative activities not only get children up and moving but also allow them to move from the abstract to the concrete in understanding the various topics. Facilitators should plan at least two activities, with a backup in case the planned ones miss the mark. As facilitators become more comfortable in leading groups they can let their creativity blossom by developing new and exciting activities to help the children gain insight and awareness.

5. Kids' Group

This session marks the one specially designated time of the day when children process and share about the learning that has taken place. The daily theme, recreation, and creative activities stir powerful feelings and emotions in the children, especially in terms of what life has been like in their families and what has been missing. Facilitators can gently guide this process by encouraging all children to share openly on a feelings level. Toward the end of the session, it is important for the facilitator to create a learning chain by recalling the daily themes and key concepts, and linking them to new information and insights gained each day.

6. Patient Group

With the support of their peers and facilitator, children are ready to openly and honestly confront their family patient in a loving and nonjudgmental way with their tough love lists. Healing occurs as family members, including children, speak from their hearts and express repressed feelings and emotions about their painful experiences. Children also receive a list from the patient that details behavior for the youngsters to look at seriously. As emotional honesty and healing transcend this experience, children later present forgiveness and reconciliation lists in an effort to forge a new beginning for themselves and hope for the family. (Youngsters briefly participate in this group three times during the week.)

7. Recreation

After a brief check-in to explore feelings and concerns about patient group, the focus returns to recreation to keep children in touch with their bodies. Because many feelings and insights have surfaced, children need vigorous yet balanced physical activity to aid them in integrating these messages consciously into their lives. Swimming is a particularly powerful exercise to facilitate this process.

8. Fun Time

The time has come to wind down the process and to provide opportunities for the children to be kids, with laughter, play, and fun. Videos, carnival games, bubbles, finger painting, and a treasure hunt complete with pirate map are all activities in which children can have fun in safe and healthy ways. Youngsters benefit from both the socialization experience and the sheer joy of being kids.

9. Closing

Group endings are equally as important as beginnings. Closure allows youngsters to wind down, feel a sense of closeness with the group, and say good-bye. It psychologically prepares children to proceed with the remainder of the day. Closings may include a brief summary from the facilitator about the day's events, a round of good-byes, and a special ritual to end the group. Such a ritual as the Serenity Prayer, a group hug, or a special song can help children remember their unique qualities, prepare them for future challenges, and remind them of the group's common bond. (See section on group closures in chapter 5.)

CHAPTER 3

Children's Program Facilitators

Facilitators' Roles and Tasks

While children's group facilitators can't solve the family problems that accompany addiction or codependency, they can nevertheless make a real difference in a child's life. By following the process outlined below, facilitators can relate to youngsters in a manner that doesn't ignore or deny the children's experiences. This approach can provide significant relief, support, and assistance to kids. Above all, it is important for facilitators to Love these children.

1. Listen

Listen to what the children are saying. Listen with your eyes. Give them focused attention with sustained eye contact and active listening. Show them that you care by entering their world and respecting what they have to say.

2. Observe

Watch for nonverbal forms of communication as well. Be aware of facial expressions, body language, and the manner in which children respond to others. Be mindful of their general appearance, who sits next to whom, and their attitude from group to group. Tone of voice also provides distinct clues about what's going on for a particular youngster.

3. Validate

Let the children know that you heard and understood what they were communicating in group. Acknowledge what was said, ask relevant and meaningful questions to show your concern, and reflect the children's feelings in a caring, nonjudgmental manner. By validating a child's perceptions and feelings, you help the youngster realize that he or she is not going crazy. (Many of these children have rarely had their perceptions and feelings validated).

4. Educate

Give children basic information about addiction and codependency in a way they can understand. Help them to realize that these family problems are not their fault and that they are not to blame. Introduce youngsters to a variety of healthy living skills, including the identification and expression of feelings, problem solving and self-care strategies, and exercises building self-worth.

5. Empower

Help children identify safe people that they may turn to for support and guidance, such as those individuals who truly care about them, are trustworthy, and aren't harmfully involved in addictive/codependent behavior. Safe people may be recovering parents, siblings, other relatives, neighbors, teachers, ministers, coaches, or counselors. Help children realize that they don't have to be alone anymore.

RESPONSIBILITIES

To effectively assist youngsters in the discovery and healing process, group facilitators need to:

• Enter the children's world

• Provide youngsters with focused attention

• Listen to what children say, both verbally and nonverbally

• Understand from the youngster's perspective

• Give children age-appropriate information they can understand

• Introduce children to a wide variety of fun and relevant activities

• Be a healthy role model to kids

• Allow youngsters to grow through their pain

• Give children options and choices to solve problems and take good care of themselves

• Respond to youngsters in a nonjudgmental way

• Constantly observe the group members' behavior in and out of group

• Develop daily plans and activities to best meet the children's needs

• Maintain a personal support system to stay healthy and have positives to give to kids

DESIRED QUALITIES

The children's program can only be as effective as the facilitators who work with youngsters week after week. Competent and compassionate individuals with a genuine love and respect for children, who understand addiction and codependency as well as its impact on kids, and who are consciously working on their own growth are the people who make effective children's facilitators. The job requires a combination of skills, knowledge, and background. Comfort in working with kids, devising daily program plans, utilizing educational objectives, and a working knowledge of child development are all essential ingredients. Understanding about addiction, codependency, and recovery skills forms another group of competencies equally important. It is the melding of these knowledge and skill areas that produces balanced and successful facilitators.

People who work in programs for children have a challenging opportunity to make a real difference. For some of the youngsters participating in the children's program, the facilitator may be the first person in whom they trust to confide their feelings. The children's program facilitator may be the first adult who has really listened to them or consistently treated them as worthwhile individuals.

With this in mind, it is important that staff members possess the following qualities:

- Love and deep caring for children
- Commitment and enthusiasm
- Overall communication skills
  Listening
  Clear communication
  Age appropriateness (simple and concise language for children)
- Overall knowledge and understanding of the issues
  Addiction
  Codependency
  Mental health problems
- Overall knowledge and experience in working with children
  Child development
  Age appropriate activities
  Session planning
  Experiential activities
- Cultural competency
- Self starter
- Responsible
- Open-minded
- Warmth
- Creative
- Flexible
- Ability to have fun
- A sense of humor
- Overall self-awareness and understanding
  Understanding of personal issues and biases
  Personal support system
  Comfort with displaying, expressing, and owning feelings
- Overall personal health
  Self-care
  Self-esteem
  Limits and boundaries
- Ability to set limits and consistently enforce consequences

CHAPTER 4

Working With Parents

The Parent Connection

Working closely with parents helps to ensure a positive experience for children during family week. Parents may come to Sierra Tucson saddled with fears, worries, and concerns about their youngsters' participation in the children's program. Staff members can alleviate much of this discomfort by explaining that the program doesn't overwhelm children, but rather meets them where they are developmentally by allowing them to be kids. Much of the work centers around fun and play. Moreover, once parents realize that we all have the same goal, healthy children, they can gradually place their support and trust in the children's program. By respectfully addressing parents' questions and concerns throughout the program, staff members not only build solid rapport with parents but also help them to realize that this is an opportunity to initiate the process of breaking the destructive family cycle of addiction, codependency, and mental health problems.

To actively facilitate a strong connection with parents, the children's program utilizes the following tools, succeeded by their examples:

1. Parent Questionnaire

This two-page history form provides background information on the family and specifically the youngster about to participate in the children's program. Filled out by parents or guardians, the questionnaire provides valuable data on the child's strengths and liabilities, as well as insight into his or her awareness and understanding of the family stresses. Parents also include their hopes about what they would like their child to gain from this experience. The parent questionnaire offers valuable information for staff members to plan and shape the weekly program and serves as the first link to directly communicating with parents during the family week process.

2. The Children's Program: Frequently Asked Questions and Answers

This two-page summary promotes direct and open communication about the children's program. In an effort to clear up any misunderstandings and erroneous assumptions, it succinctly sketches the scope and focus of the program and addresses commonly asked questions by parents about their children's participation. Above all, this information attempts to get everyone on the same wave length about exactly what the children's program offers in the way of help and healing for youngsters.

3. Release Forms

Signed by parents (or guardians) prior to their child's participation in the program, this document gives youngsters permission to participate in all children's program activities, including hiking and swimming. It also provides legal authorization to treat a minor in the very unlikely event of accident or illness.

4. Welcome Letter to Children

Included in the family packet sent home with the preceding three items, this letter specifically welcomes children to the upcoming journey on which they are about to embark. Designed to clarify any misconceptions they might have about the children's program, it stresses how the program balances fun with learning. The letter also invites youngsters to call children's program staff members with any questions or concerns they might have about coming to Sierra Tucson. Most of all, it lets kids know they are important and welcome here.

5. Children's Program Daily Schedule

Given to parents and other family members on Monday morning as part of the children's program orientation, the daily schedule features a broad overview of the weekly program for kids. It provides such useful information as the daily themes and times for program activities, and outlines important requirements (i.e., all youngsters must be accompanied by an adult during free time on campus). All adult family members who have a youngster participating in the children's program should receive a copy of the schedule so that they can familiarize themselves with the program.

6. Follow up meeting

Parents are encouraged to meet with children's program staff members on Friday afternoon to receive feedback about their youngsters' progress during the week. At this time parents are informed of the healthy strides their children have made during the week, as well as areas of concern that may require further exploration and assistance. Often specific continuing care recommendations are provided to meet the individual needs of each child. This is also a time for parents to address any questions or concerns they may have about their children.

PARENT QUESTIONNAIRE
Sierra Tucson Children's Program

Dear Parent,

Please provide the following information to help make your child's experience here a nurturing and healing one. Add any other important information on the back of these sheets. This information is confidential and only Sierra Tucson Staff will have access to it.

Thanks,

Jerry Moe, M.A.
Children's Program Manager

Child's Name _____ Birth date _____

Street Address _____ City _____

State_____ Zip Code_____ Grade in School _____

Names/Ages of other children in the family _____

Addiction/Codependency History: Name of patient in treatment _____

Patient is in treatment for _____

Family history of addiction/codependency(list persons and their addictions): _____
_____

Is your child aware of why the patient is at Sierra Tucson and what the patient's addictions are?_____

Is the child aware of other family members' addictions? _____
_____

Are any family members in recovery? If so, how long? _____
_____

What is the history of the parent relationship (married, separated, divorced, single, remarried)?
_____

If separated or divorced, who has child custody? _____

How frequent is visitation with the non-custodial parent?_____

What concerns relate directly to your child? _____

Is there any abuse or fear of incest? _____

Does the child have problems in school?_____
_____

Does the child have health problems? Currently taking any medication? _____

Stomachaches, headaches, sleeping or eating problems?_____

Any major life changes within the past year for your child (death, separation, moves, etc.) _____

_____

_____

What would you like from this program? What current issues need exploration? _____

_____

Has your child ever participated in a support group?_____

Counseling/therapy? _____

Other comments you'd like children's program staff to know to better assist your child:

Person filling out this form_____

Relationship to child _____

THE CHILDREN'S PROGRAM
FREQUENTLY ASKED QUESTIONS AND ANSWERS—
Sierra Tucson Children's Program

Dear Parents,

Here are the answers to commonly asked questions about the children's program. I look forward to serving you and your children.

Jerry Moe

Jerry Moe, M.A.
Children's Program Manager

What information is presented to children?

The children's program introduces youngsters to a variety of healthy living skills, such as the identification and expression of feelings, a variety of problem solving, coping, and self-care strategies, and exercises designed to build self-esteem and self-worth. The program also teaches children about addiction and codependency in an age-appropriate way. Empowering youngsters with life skills, the children's program is primary prevention in action.

Will a child who is thirteen-years-old automatically be put in the adult group or is there flexibility?

The children's program is designed to serve youngsters between the ages of six and twelve. While this seems to work best for most children, the program strives to meet the individual needs of each child. Staff members occasionally determine that a thirteen-year-old would best be served in the children's program, while in other cases a teenager's maturity and developmental level are way beyond the scope of the program. In rare cases a five-and-a-half-year-old can benefit from the children's program, although it's difficult for most children at this age to actively participate for eight hours daily.

Are my children going to be told why their family member is in treatment?

The children's program stresses the value and importance of each child being given the opportunity to be a kid. Sometimes family secrets, many of which the children are at least partially aware, hinder this process. During family week the patient will be encouraged by staff members to let his or her children know why they are in treatment. Counselors will assist in how to disclose this information in an age-appropriate manner that children can understand and handle, all in an attempt to preserve their childhood and to free them from confusion and taking responsibility for family problems.

Will my child be put in a group with kids whose parents are alcoholics or drug addicts?

Youngsters participating in the children's program have parents or other family members in treatment at Sierra Tucson for a variety of problems, such as addiction, codependency, and/or mental health concerns. The common bonds these children experience are family problems and stress. In the program children can talk about these problems, share their feelings, learn new ways to take care of themselves, and come to feel better about themselves.

Do the children have play time and breaks during the day?

Because the program stresses the importance of being a kid, plenty of time is scheduled for play and breaks throughout the day. Almost all of the breaks coincide with family program breaks, so parents have ample opportunity to check-in with their kids. The children's program provides a balanced blend of recreation, play, and educational support activities, all of which are done primarily through play, puppets, music, movement, art, stories, role-plays, and specially designed games. Most children enjoy their time in the program and learn valuable and healing skills along the way.

Will the children's program counselor meet with the parents to discuss their children's behaviors and/or problems?

Children's program staff members are available on a daily basis to address any issues or concerns parents may have. Please make appointments as needed. After graduation on Friday afternoon, the children's program counselor is available to discuss children's progress during the week, any problem areas or concerns, and continuing care recommendations. Again, make an appointment to get this extremely valuable feedback and information.

SIERRA TUCSON COMPANIES, INC
Release

Name of participant   Age   Sex

Name of parent or guardian

Street address   City   State   Zip

Name of Emergency Contact   (Relationship)   Phone

I am aware that participation in Sierra Tucson's Children's program involves certain activities (such as swimming and hiking) which are physically demanding and potentially dangerous for children. Therefore, as a participant, my child must be free of medical or physical conditions which might create undue risk. I understand that physical strength is not necessary, although being in good physical condition will increase enjoyment of the activities.

I am aware that these activities involve a potential risk for illness and injury to my child and property. I acknowledge that I am aware of and assume all risks and wish to allow my child to participate in the activities. As part of the consideration for my child's participation at Sierra Tucson, I agree to assume full responsibility for any loss, injury or inconvenience that my child might suffer. To the extent that I participate in such activities, I do so voluntarily and assume any and all risk of injury to my person or property resulting therefrom. I further agree to indemnify and hold harmless Sierra Tucson, Inc. and all its subsidiaries and officers from any and all liability incurred as a result of participation by myself or my child. I also agree that the terms hereof shall serve as a release and assumption of risk for my heirs, executors and administrators, and for all members of my family.

Signature (Parent/legal guardian must sign for persons under 18)   Date

Medical Information: It is necessary for us to know if your child has any medical considerations. If not, please write "no"; if so, please write "yes" and describe in detail and send any medications to Sierra Tucson. You may write long answers on the back of the form.

Chronic medical condition: (i.e. diabetes, asthma, seizures, etc.):

Allergic reactions to: (i.e. insect bites/stings or poison oak or medication)

Any surgery, sprained muscles or broken bones within the past 12 months?

Authorization to treat a minor: In the event I cannot be reached in an emergency, I hereby give permission to the person named as emergency contact to authorize medical and hospital care of my child, and if such person cannot be contacted, I give permission to the physician selected by Sierra Tucson to hospitalize, secure proper treatment for, and to order injections, anesthesia, or surgery for my child as named above.

Signature (Parent/legal guardian must sign for persons under 18)   Date

WELCOME LETTER TO CHILDREN

Dear Friend,

I am excited and happy that you will soon be coming to Sierra Tucson for family week. My name is Jerry and I'll be working with you in the children's program. Most of the kids who come here just call me "Jellybeans."

I bet you wonder what you are going to do here. In the children's program we have lots of fun. We do some work, too, like sharing about our feelings and learning new ways to take care of ourselves. Above all, you will learn here that you are a STAR. You are one-of-a-kind, that's pretty special. During the week we might use puppets, art, movies, and stories to help us.

There's lots more. Maybe we'll take a short hike, play a fun game, or shoot some hoops. Remember to pack some sunscreen, a bathing suit, and a favorite stuffed animal if you would like.

When I think about you coming, I feel happy and excited. I can't wait to meet you and be your friend.

See you soon,

Jerry Moe

Jerry

P.S. If you have any questions, give me a call. My telephone number is 800-624-9001. Ask for Jerry in the children's program.

CHILDREN'S PROGRAM DAILY SCHEDULE

The children's program offers education, support and fun for youngsters between the ages of six and twelve. This program meets every day of family week. The daily themes for the children are:

MONDAY	**Not My Fault**	(Family Addiction and Codependency)
TUESDAY	**All My Feelings Are Okay**	(Feelings)
WEDNESDAY	**Taking Care of Me**	(Problem Solving and Self-care)
THURSDAY	**I Am Special**	(Self-worth)
FRIDAY	**Celebrate Me**	(Good-byes and Hellos)

The children's program schedule is as follows:

MONDAY

8:15 - 9:45 am	Children's Program
10:00 - 10:15 am	Break
10:15 - 11:45 am	Family Group w/ Family Member
11:45 - 12:45 pm	Lunch w/ Family
12:45 - 4:30 pm	Children's Program

TUESDAY & THURSDAY

8:15 - 9:45 am	Children's Program
10:00 - 10:15 am	Break w/ C.P. Staff
10:15 - 11:45 am	Children's Program
11:45 - 12:45 pm	Lunch w/ Family
12:45 - 1:30 pm	Family/Patient Group
1:30 - 4:30 pm	Children's Program

WEDNESDAY

8:15 - 9:45 am	Children's Program
10:00 - 10:15 am	Break w/ C.P. Staff
10:15 - 11:45 am	Children's Program
11:45 - 12:45 pm	Lunch w/ Family
12:45 - 4:30 pm	Children's Program

FRIDAY

8:15 - 9:45 am	Children's Program
10:00 - 10:15 am	Break w/ C.P. Staff
10:15 - 11:45 am	Children's Program

Please note the following:

- All children's groups take place in the Children's Room. Once the children become familiar with its location, they are expected to arrive at the scheduled times.
- Pick up your children at the end of each day at the Children's Room.
- Children must be accompanied by an adult at all times on Sierra Tucson premises. Parents are responsible for their children at all times when they are not in the children's group.
- The children's program features art, puppets, music, movement, role plays, story telling, games, and play to assist youngsters in the healing process.

Please contact me if you have any questions or concerns.

Jerry Moe

Jerry Moe, M.A., Children's Program Manager

CHAPTER 5

Children's Program Nuts and Bolts

Group Rules and Consequences

Bring together a group of children, most of whom will be new to one another, to create an environment where they feel willing and safe to share their thoughts and feelings is a major undertaking. The majority of these children probably will have never participated in a group before. They will be unaccustomed to and unfamiliar with the boundaries and expectations of the support group process. Group rules and consistently enforced consequences when the rules are violated ensure the participants' safety and afford them the dignity and respect they deserve.

In establishing group rules and consequences, the following guidelines may be considered:

1. Keep group rules simple so youngsters can clearly understand them.

2. Keep rules to a minimum. Trust that the group process will take care of many problem areas, especially once children are empowered with "when you, I feel" statements.

3. To impart healthy living skills, form the rules as positive statements. Youngsters will respond much better to positive rules than they will to those that just seem to get them into trouble. For example, "Respect each other" is a very different and much more positive rule than "Don't hit, don't kick, and don't hurt each other."

4. Consistently enforce the rules. Follow through with appropriate consequences each time a rule is violated. This is vital to ensuring the group's safety and well-being.

5. Make sure you are comfortable with the consequences so you can administer them if rules do get broken.

6. Set a positive example by following these rules.

Clearly print the rules and consequences on a greaseboard or on posterboard and display them in the group room. At the start of each day, review them and make sure the group members understand each and every one. Doing so consistently helps not only to remind youngsters that they are safe in group but also that the rules serve to protect them.

Make certain the children understand that the rules apply to the facilitators as well.

The following group rules and consequences are suggested for the children's program at Sierra Tucson:

GROUP RULES

1. One person talks at a time.

2. Respect one another.

3. Put-ups only.

4. You can pass.

5. What we say here stays here.

CONSEQUENCES

Coming to the children's program is like playing baseball, three strikes and you're out. Each day is like a new time at bat; it starts with no strikes on anyone. When someone breaks a rule, the facilitators may give him or her a strike.

Strike One: A warning

Strike Two: A five-to-ten minute time-out

Strike Three: Set up a conference*

The most important rule in the children's program is confidentiality, "What we say here stays here." Youngsters talk more freely and share feelings more openly when they believe what they say will not get spread around or told directly to their parents. In reviewing the rules daily, always inform children of the one exception to the confidentiality rule: "If you share in group that someone is hurting you or touching you inappropriately, I may have to report that information to help you stay safe. If I do so, I will let you know about it."

Even though children rarely violate the confidentiality rule, it is so vital to the success of the children's program that it must always be stressed and never compromised.

Group Openers

One or more of the following questions can be used at the beginning of a group meeting to break the ice and encourage kids to share their thoughts and feelings:

• What is your favorite day of the year?

---

* The purpose of the conference is to determine if the children's program best meets the child's needs. The children's facilitator, family counselor, children's program manager, the child, and his or her parents may attend this meeting. The outcome may be that the youngster remains in the program, receives some individual counseling, spends the rest of family week at the day care, or some combination. Above all, the needs of each child are particularly addressed.

- If you had all the money in the world, what would you do?
- What famous person would you like to meet?
- What kind of food would you be on a cold day?
- What's one thing you'd like to be remembered for?
- What kind of animal do you feel like today?
- Who are your heroes?
- If you could only have one wish, what would you wish for?
- What is your favorite movie?
- What's a topic you have difficulty talking about?
- What is something you find really funny?
- What is one of your special qualities?
- What food do you think is gross?
- What do you like to do for fun?
- If you could do anything you want tomorrow, what would you do?
- What is the best gift you've given someone?
- What feeling is easy for you to share?
- What would you like to be famous for?
- What kind of animal would you like to be?
- What would you like to be doing ten years from now?
- What subject would you like to teach others?
- If you could have one wish to improve your family, what would you wish for?
- If you could have cartoon characters for parents, who would your Dad be?
- If you could have cartoon characters for parents, who would your Mom be?
- If you could go anywhere on an adventure, where would you go?
- What's something you would like to learn more about?
- Who is a safe person you can talk to?
- If you could spend the day with a famous person, what would you do?
- What special quality would you like to have?
- What feeling is difficult for you to express?
- Where is a safe place you can go?

Group Closers

The following activities help the group wind down and provide a transition for closure. They also empower youngsters with strategies and important messages to assist them until the group meets again.

• Paragraph Giraffe

The facilitator writes the words, "Today in group, we . . ." on the greaseboard or newsprint. Every group member has the opportunity to add a sentence which fits the sentence that precedes it. Giggles, laughter, and a serious case of the "sillies" often abound.

- **The Serenity Prayer**

God grant me the serenity to accept the things I cannot change, the courage to change the things I can, and the wisdom to know the difference.

- **Rainbow**

Sitting in a circle, everyone shares their hopes and dreams, specifically what their "pot of gold" at the end of the rainbow looks like.

- **Hand Squeeze**

With the group standing in a circle and holding hands with one another, the facilitator begins by gently squeezing the hand of the person on his or her right. The squeeze then continues around the circle of children.

- **Fun Factory**

Group members share something fun they hope to do before the next group.

- **Car Wash**

(See activities under Thursday: I AM SPECIAL for a description of this exercise.)

- **Group Hug**

Everyone stands in a circle and places their arms on the shoulders of the persons on each side. Everyone gently gives a squeeze on the shoulders.

- **Gifts Galore**

Sitting in a circle, everyone gives a special "gift" to the person on their left, such as the gift of playfulness, the gift of understanding, the gift of love, the gift of joy, etc..

- **Joke Time**

Members have the chance to share a joke or two.

- **Song**

Some groups adopt a particular song as the group song. You can either play the song or have the group sing it.

- **Affirmation Sensation**

(See activities under Thursday: I AM SPECIAL for a description of this exercise.)

Dealing With Suspected Abuse

Before you initiate working with children, review your program's policies and procedures for reporting cases of suspected child abuse. Children's program staff members are mandated by law to report all such suspected cases. Because this can be an emotionally distressing and draining experience, it is imperative to follow the established policies and procedures, as well as to activate your own support system.

As a children's program staff member it may come to your attention either directly or indirectly that a child is being physically or sexually abused. Pay close attention to youngsters exhibiting the following signs, all of which may be indicative of abuse:

- Fear of being touched
- Consistent wearing of jackets, long-sleeve shirts, and long pants, regardless of the temperature
- Unexplainable or oddly placed bruises
- Undue fear of parents or other adults
- Excessive fearfulness for or protectiveness of younger siblings
- Inappropriate seductive or sexual behavior

Always trust your instincts. If your suspicions become aroused for some reason or a child discloses information during a group, meet privately with the youngster to discuss your concerns. While group isn't the appropriate place to discuss the individual circumstances of abuse, it is appropriate to inform group members that abuse is a serious matter and that you will act on it.

If you need to meet individually with a child, let the youngster know that he or she isn't in trouble. Emphasize that you care very much about his or her safety and well-being. Avoid making promises that you can't keep ("This will never happen again"). Obtain the basic facts and, if necessary, notify the appropriate staff to set up a child abuse meeting.

Guidelines For Dealing With Suspected Abuse

Here are some guidelines to follow in dealing with cases of suspected abuse:

1. If a child discloses any information about possible abuse (keep in mind that neglect is a form of abuse), meet with the youngster individually after group. Make every effort to gain the child's trust and confidence, and let the youngster know he or she is not in trouble. Make it clear that the goal of the children's program is to help the child stay safe.

2. Ask the child for specific information about what had been previously disclosed (e.g., What specifically happened? Does that occur frequently? Have you ever had bruises, hand marks, or burns on your body as a result of getting in trouble or being hit?). Get specific data when you ask the child what has happened. For example, a specific statement would be, "My grandfather puts his hands on my private parts." You might ask, "Is this with your clothes on or off?" Don't ask for graphic details.

3. Notify the appropriate staff members about the situation. This will provide an opportunity to discuss the case.

4. Set up a child abuse meeting to discuss the case and to determine if a report should be filed. No children's program staff member needs to make such a determination alone. This can be a team decision, and the facilitator involved can get the assistance of fellow staff members.

5. All reports to Children's Protective Services must be followed up with a written report within 36 hours. Have the necessary forms available in case you need to make a report.

6. Let the child know you are making a report. Show your concern. Let the youngster know you want to help him or her stay safe.

7. A report is filed when child abuse is suspected. Children's program staff members are not responsible for investigating such matters. The proper authorities will follow up on the report.

8. Filing a report can be a scary and emotionally distressing experience. It is essential for children's program staff members to lend support to one another when such a situation arises.

Program Planning

A successful group experience in the children's program largely hinges on thorough planning done in advance. It may be helpful to keep a notebook of lesson plans. Sketch out the various segments of each day on separate pages. After reading the patients' psych-social histories and the questionnaires filled out by the parents about their children, you'll have a clearer idea of what daily key concepts to present, as well as which games and activities to use to convey those concepts. Copy the lesson plan on an index card and keep it handy to refer to during the day. After some time in the children's program, you'll have an accurate sense of the needs of the group and what kind of activities might work best for them.

Here are some helpful hints to assist you in planning daily activities for the children's program:

1. Each daily theme provides several key concepts to focus on throughout the day. To assist you in dealing with the wide developmental span of youngsters in the program from week to week, choose the concepts you deem most appropriate for each particular group. Since trying to present too much material only results in confusion, err on the side of simplicity, as one or two concepts per day usually suffices.

2. Now decide what activities will bring the key concepts to life. Good activities not only get youngsters up and moving, but also result in deeper understanding and meaning. In time, let your own creativity blossom by developing new and exciting ways to help children learn and grow.

3. Choose rich and varied activities, including art, film, discussion, and movement. Youngsters learn in a variety of ways, visually, auditorily, kinesthetically. Games and activities incorporating these learning styles allow you to reach more children.

4. Always enter the children's world and join them in the process. If children sit together on the floor, sit with them. If they are working on a collage project, take part in the activity. This participation communicates to the children that the activities are valuable for everyone, children and adults alike.

5. Make sure that your lesson plans fit the allotted time. Always maintain a steady pace, one that neither bores nor overwhelms children. Be flexible in adjusting your plans as necessary.

6. Have fun. Allow the children to be kids, to have fun and learn at the same time.

7. With the above guidelines in mind, remember that your purpose is to meet the youngsters' needs. While daily structure and consistency promote bonding and trust, flexibility is paramount when working with children. Comforting a child in a moment of need and steering toward a new course of focus may take precedence over the lesson plan on occasion. Being able to adapt to these changing needs of children is essential to a facilitator's success.

PART 2

Daily Activities

Not My Fault — Family Addiction and Codependency

KEY CONCEPTS
- Addiction and codependency are a family disease. Everyone in the family gets hurt by it.
- Family addiction and codependency are not my fault.
- I am at high risk for addictions and codependency.

GOALS
- To increase knowledge and understanding of addiction and codependency.
- To learn that children didn't cause and can't control or cure family addiction and codependency.
- To understand that children are at high risk for addiction and codependency, because these problems tend to run in families.
- To help children realize they are not alone, many kids live in families with addiction and codependency problems.

ACTIVITIES

The Addiction Game

Letters to the Disease

Bicycle

Bubble Gum Family

Addiction Illustrated

Rad Ads

The Disease Game

Bicycle II

Treatment-n-Recovery

Rock-n-Roll Recovery

High-Risk Me

Can't Cure It Game

Dear Gabby

Stuck in the Feelings Redux

High-Risk Me, Too

Tough Love Lists

BOOKS/STORIES   *My House is Different*

Pepper

The Brown Bottle

"Ms. Piggy's Secret" (In *Kids Are Special* curriculum)

"The Night before the County Fair" (In *Kids Are Special* curriculum)

FILMS   *The Cat Who Drank Too Much*

Twee, Fiddle, and Huff

Lots of Kids Like Us

Francesca Baby

She Drinks a Little

Just Tipsy Honey

All Bottled Up

A Story About Feelings

SONGS   "No Excuse T' Use Booze" by Peter Alsop (*Stayin' Over* cassette)

"There's An Elephant In The Living Room" by Jim Newton (*Children at Heart* cassette)

DAILY THEME   Mini-Lecture

Children living in addicted and/or codependent families often think they are the only ones in their school or neighborhood who have such family problems. They may feel quite confused about what is happening in their homes. Even those insightful youngsters who realize that alcohol or other drugs are a major problem in their families usually lack a basic understanding about this disease. Consequently, many get the idea that the situation is somehow all their fault and this notion gets compounded by the cloak of secrecy and silence that predominates in their home environment. Such thoughts as, "If I only did more work around the house," "If I wouldn't fight so much with my brother and sister," "If I only got better grades at school," or "If I could only be a better kid," progressively occupy these children daily. With time, guilt and shame can steadily consume these youngsters in a vicious cycle of don't talk, don't feel, and don't trust. When attempts to solve the problems and make everything better ultimately fail, children are left with even more guilt and shame.

To combat these tendencies, explain the basics about the family disease of addiction and codependency. Help the children to understand how it affects everyone in a family, including the kids. Youngsters experience incredible relief when they learn that the problems are not their fault and that they are not alone, as there are many families and children dealing with similar situations.

Begin with a discussion about alcohol and other drugs. Describe people who have an illness or disease called addiction, and how these individuals get stuck, hooked, and controlled by chemicals. As a result, their feelings get confused and they can't take good care of themselves and those they love. While the drugs temporarily change their feelings, their true feelings build up and hide inside. More and more problems accumulate as the chemicals actually run the addicts' lives. Often the very qualities that make these people so very special get completely lost in the disease. Despite all of this the addicted persons can't stop because the disease controls all aspects of their lives. These people are ill and can only recover when they seek the help of others.

Help children to understand that people can get hooked on a variety of things. Add food, tobacco, work, gambling, and relationships as other things people get hooked on, all in an attempt to change their feelings. Also introduce the concept of codependency here, emphasizing how some people get hooked by always taking care of and trying to control others. Codependents also have difficulty taking good care of themselves, sharing their real feelings, and staying in touch with their special qualities.

After outlining these basics, describe how everyone in a family is affected by addiction and/or codependency. Listing common problems in such a family helps youngsters to realize that fighting, hurt feelings, tension, broken promises, lack of attention, family secrets, embarrassment, yelling and raging, and frequent accidents and illnesses often occur in addicted/codependent families. Explain that trying to hide the disease or pretend it isn't there only prolongs the problems and makes matters worse. Above all, help children learn the 5 *C*'s when it comes to family addiction and/or codependency problems.

I didn't *C*ause it. (Kids can't make someone have this disease.)

I can't *C*ontrol it. (Addicts/codependents must get help for themselves.)

I can't *C*ure it. (Addicts/codependents need special help to get better and only if they want to get better.)

But I can learn to *C*ope with it by taking good *C*are of myself.

Briefly introduce youngsters to the concept of recovery. Help them to realize the importance of taking good care of themselves, especially because addiction and codependency tend to run in families.

The Addiction Game
(Ages 6 and up)

The Addiction Game helps youngsters come to a new understanding of the disease concept of addiction. Using both a visual and kinesthetic format, this activity enables youngsters to differentiate between the person they love and care about and the disease that consumes and overtakes that person. An extremely powerful exercise, it demonstrates that addiction is not the children's fault and that they are powerless to make it all better.

DESCRIPTION

The group facilitator asks for a youngster to role-play the dependent person in this game. The facilitator role-plays the disease of addiction. Starting with alcohol and other drugs, the disease makes all kinds of promises to the dependent if only that person would drink or use a little, "I'll make all your problems go away. I'll get rid of all your uncomfortable feelings. I'll make you more popular, funny, strong, and better looking." The dependent gradually gives in and begins using the chemicals. At first it appears that the disease really is becoming a good friend to the dependent.

After a short while the disease sneaks up on the dependent and quickly grabs him or her by the arms. Despite repeated struggling and pleading, the person is hooked and the disease simply won't let go. A discussion ensues about how the disease is now totally in charge of the person's life. The group talks about how none of the promises ever come true, how the person is trapped, and how problems and uncomfortable feelings accumulate instead of going away. The dependent shares how he or she feels to be so stuck. Typical responses range from scared and hopeless to angry and totally helpless.

An option here is to invite other children to try to free the "stuck family member." Youngsters struggle physically, beg and plead, make empty threats, and try all sorts of means to get the dependent unstuck, all to no avail. Through this added activity children understand that the addiction is not their fault and they can't make it better. Perhaps for the first time youngsters can separate the person they love from the disease they've come to despise and hate.

EXAMPLE

Rhonda harbored intense anger and sadness over her mother's recent cocaine relapse. By playing the dependent she quickly experienced how helpless her mother became and how the disease totally ran her life. "I really understand how sick my Mom becomes. She's out of control." With tears streaming down her face Rhonda uttered, "I love my Mom but I'm still mad at her for getting sick again. But I really hate this disease. It takes Mom away. I really hate it." Somehow this activity helped Rhonda to realize the difference between her mom and her mom's addiction.

"It's not my fault. I can't make it better."

"I'm not alone. Lots of kids deal with this problem daily."

"All my feelings are okay."

Repeat this exercise until all the youngsters have had an opportunity to kinesthetically experience how it feels to be addicted.

Use other substances or processes for youngsters to get hooked on, cigarettes, food, gambling, work, taking care of others (codependency), and relationships all can be stressed here.

Letters to the Disease
(Ages 7 and up)

An excellent follow-up to the Addiction Game, this exercise allows youngsters to express deep-seated feelings about the disease that has created many of their families' problems. Writing a letter facilitates the process of helping children realize their powerlessness over family addiction and/or codependency. It also provides a gateway for kids to initiate their own recovery by taking good care of themselves. (See the sample letter at the end of this section.)

DESCRIPTION

Based on the graphic illustrations of the Addiction Game (where youngsters can clearly differentiate between their loved ones and the disease that consumes them), this activity begins when the facilitator gives each group member a piece of paper with the words "Dear Addiction" at the top of the page. The facilitator instructs the children to write a letter to the disease that has hooked their loved ones so completely. Reassuring the children that no one outside the group will ever see these letters, the facilitator tells them to find a comfortable spot in the room to do their writing. The facilitator roams around the room and offers youngsters support and encouragement as they complete this task.

Children quite often express anger, hurt, sadness, fear, guilt, and shame. They describe the problems that have overwhelmed their loved ones, as well as their families. The group facilitator may give the youngsters the option of sharing their letters with the group if they so desire. After taking a day to discuss the letters and the feelings that developed as a result of them, the group can symbolically burn or bury these letters to let their feelings go.

EXAMPLE

Jimmy, a shy and withdrawn twelve-year-old, approached his letter writing with unusual vigor. He unfurled a barrage of anger at the disease that stuck his parents. Jimmy also expressed fear that it could happen to him, "I am scared this nightmare might happen to me when I grow up. I don't want it to but I'm scared it will trap me too." At this point Jimmy quietly cried tears he had been storing for quite some time. He received much love and support from the group as he released these pent-up feelings.

AFFIRMATIONS

"All my feelings are okay."

"I can express my feelings honestly, even my anger and fear."

"The disease is not my fault."

"My parents really do love me, but they are ill and might not always be able to show it."

COMMENTS

Help younger children write their letters by providing some assistance with general ideas and spelling.

Even if youngsters choose not to read their letters to the group, a general discussion of the feelings that surfaced during the writing brings children relief in knowing they are not alone in their family problems and feelings.

Help youngsters make the connection between sharing feelings and then letting go of them by burning or burying their letters. This assists youngsters in understanding they can share anger without hurting themselves or others.

MATERIALS

- "Dear Addiction" work sheets

- Pencils

Example of letter to the disease.

Dear Alcoholism & Drugs
Why did you pick my family?
Why won't you let go of my dad,
My dad will probably die because of
you! He has already lost his drivers
license from drunk driving. He can't
come to see me unless he is lucky
enough to get a ride.
I can't live with my mom because
of you! I hardly get to see my
parents. I can't even call my mom
because she can't afford a phone,

I Hate You!

Signed
a VERY ANGRY Kid

Bicycle
(Ages 4 and up)

This exercise provides children with a hands-on experiential process that not only captures their imaginations but also focuses on the reality of the disease. Children see and feel how the bicycle ride symbolizes addiction and a loss of control. They gain fundamental understanding of this family disease and have fun while doing so.

DESCRIPTION Begin the activity by telling the children that they are going to take a ride on an octocycle (assuming there are eight kids and eight chairs). Each child represents a family member, with the alcoholic/addict steering at the front. An invisible bar connects each seat to emphasize the rigidness and enmeshment of the disease. Children sit in their chairs and make the circular motion of bicycle pedals with their arms and hands. By reading a story (see "Bicycle Ride Narrative"), the facilitator takes the children for a ride. An initially peaceful, joyful journey gradually turns into a rainstorm on a steep downhill grade. Suddenly, no brakes! Crash!

After the crash the facilitator asks the children questions about the experience.

EXAMPLE Nine-year-old Danielle summed up the experience best: "The bike ride was fun at first but scary at the end. Alcoholics don't have brakes when it comes to drinking. I guess relapse is when they think they have brakes even though they don't."

AFFIRMATIONS "I don't have to go on the alcoholic ride. I can get help."

"I can make helpful choices to stay safe."

"It's not my fault; I don't have to be alone anymore."

COMMENTS The exercise also helps children bring the disease to conscious reality by talking about their feelings.

Learning that the disease is not their fault and brainstorming ways of taking care of themselves are made possible by this game.

MATERIALS • Bicycle Ride Narrative
• Chairs

BICYCLE RIDE NARRATIVE

"Okay, everybody in position.

"We are going for a nice ride through the country. It's a beautiful day. The sun is shining and the grass is green. There's no wind, just a gentle, warm breeze. We are pedaling slowly, breathing evenly, enjoying the scenery, and chatting and laughing with one another. We put on the brakes slowly as a dog wags his way across our path.

"As we gather speed a few dark clouds begin to appear over the horizon, the breeze becomes a little stiffer, and the smooth pavement turns into a dirt road. We begin to pedal a little harder and grab the handlebars a little tighter. The clouds are becoming darker and some light rain begins to fall. The dirt road is getting slippery and bumpy. We keep putting on the brakes but continue moving. We have to lean forward and pedal harder to go up a hill. Our legs and stomachs are sore, and our hands grab the handlebars even tighter. The rain is coming down faster and at times the bike almost tips over.

"We reach the top of the hill exhausted but it is raining so hard we have to keep moving. We start pedaling faster as we go down the other side of the hill. The rain is slapping harder onto our faces. The bike is sliding back and forth across the road. Loud sounds of thunder can be heard. Lightning strikes a tree near us. We are pedaling faster and faster, and holding on tighter and tighter. Our feet keep slipping and we try the brakes. The brakes don't hold, they no longer work. We're losing control. The pedals are spinning at full speed. The road is much steeper and bumpier as we go even faster, trying the brakes (still no brakes) and holding on for dear life. CRASH, the bike tips over!"

Bicycle Questions

1. What was the ride like for you?

2. How was this like alcoholism/addiction?

3. How was this like what you experience in your own home?

4. Was everyone affected?

5. When you fell down, who did you have to help first?

6. What would you do if the alcoholic/chemical dependent wanted to get back on the bike and continue down the hill?

7. Whose fault is it?

8. Where can you go to get help?

This activity is taken from *Kids' Power: Healing Games for Children of Alcoholics.*

Bubble Gum Family
(Ages 6 and up)

In a simple yet powerful way, Bubble Gum Family helps children understand what happens to everyone in a family struggling with addiction and codependency. Frequently used as a demonstration during community education sessions on how to work with young children of addiction, this activity helps children of all ages learn and have fun in the process.

DESCRIPTION

Almost everyone has had some experience chewing bubble gum. What's your favorite brand? Remember how sticky it becomes after a few quick chews if you take it out of your mouth? Yuck! Have you ever had a big wad of gum stuck on the bottom of your shoe?

In this game everyone imagines there are 9,997 pieces of slightly chewed bubble gum in an imaginary circle on the floor. Children volunteer to role-play an addicted parent, the spouse, and several children. Using a narrative the facilitator orchestrates a scenario in which everyone in the family gets stuck in the addiction (bubble gum).

First the addicted parent gets stuck by using alcohol and other drugs. The spouse and children get stuck in their attempts to help the addicted parent. Once stuck in the gum everyone has a hard time moving. They lose choice in what they think and do. Only by first taking good care of themselves can family members get unstuck. Different strategies for taking good care of oneself and the progression of the disease are stressed.

EXAMPLE

This activity allowed Jim, age twelve, to understand how he impedes his mother's recovery by constantly taking care of her. Jim and three others played the roles of his father and siblings. Jim's mom was stuck in the center, and the rest of the family got stuck trying to help her. We instructed Jim and the others to circle very closely around his mom. Then we asked Mom to come out of the bubble gum. Jim said, "Even if she wanted to, she couldn't move because everyone else is in the way trying to take care of her. Boy, I guess it's true that if I take care of me, I give Mom the space to do the same for herself. I think I understand it now but it's hard to let go of her. I guess it begins with me."

AFFIRMATIONS

"I can trust my feelings to help me know what's best."

COMMENTS

Allow children the opportunity to role-play various family members. This lets them see how everyone becomes stuck in similar ways.

Process feelings and discuss how this exercise is similar to the children's family experiences.

MATERIALS

Bubble Gum Family Narrative

BUBBLE GUM FAMILY NARRATIVE

"We're going to do an activity now called Bubble Gum Family. Almost everyone has chewed bubble gum. There are all different kinds of bubblegum that people chew: Hubba Bubba, Carefree, Bazooka, or Bubble Yum Bubblegum are just a few of the brands that you can choose from.

"Have you ever chewed bubble gum for about thirty seconds and then taken it out of your mouth? How does it feel? It's real sticky and yucky. Here in the middle of the floor is an imaginary circle. We've stayed up the past twenty-four hours and chewed piece after piece of bubble gum, each for thirty seconds. Then we have thrown it into our imaginary circle. Here in this circle are 9,997 pieces of slightly chewed bubble gum.

"Here we have a family. 'Miss, please come up.' I want the rest of you to meet Tammy. She is thirty-five years old, a mother of three, a wonderful mom. She has a full-time job. Just an incredible lady. Since she's been a young adult, Tammy has gone out each weekend to drink with her friends, but it doesn't seem to have been a problem. All of a sudden as Tammy is going through life, she steps right in the bubble gum. She's stuck. 'Try to move, Tammy.'

"'Well, I'm trying, but I can't really move too much.'

"That's right, you can't move too much. That's addiction. People get stuck. Watch Tammy. She can sway from side to side. She really thinks she's not stuck, that she can get out of that really quickly, but she can't."

"What happens as time goes on is that Tammy becomes more and more preoccupied with the gum while she's stuck in it. She isn't doing as good a job at work. She's out sick a lot. She isn't as productive because she's preoccupied with the gum. It's really starting to slow her down. She doesn't have freedom of choice anymore. When it comes to her kids, she can't take care of them like she used to. She's trapped in that gum. She's stuck! She's not spending as much time with her kids. She prepares dinner and just goes off on her own.

"Tammy has a husband named Fred. Fred loves his wife very much. Fred's been very concerned about Tammy. 'Haven't you, Fred?'

"'Why, yes.'

"Fred has been concerned because he notices his wife is stuck in the gum. She's on probation at work because she has been absent so many days. Her last review wasn't very good. Fred has noticed over the past few months that he has had to take on more and more of the responsibilities at home. He's starting to prepare dinner. Fred is also spending time helping the kids with their homework and helping them with their projects on the weekend. He's very concerned about his wife. He doesn't get to spend as much time with her alone because she seems preoccupied and distant. She's just stuck in that gum.

"Because Fred cares for and loves his wife, what do you suppose he tries to do? He tries to free his wife from the bubble gum. 'So go ahead, Fred, go and try to help your wife.'

"As Fred tries to help his wife, he gets stuck in the bubble gum too. 'Try to move around, Fred.' Notice, he thinks he can move around and he thinks he's free, but he's really stuck. Remember that addiction is a progressive disease. When Tammy first got stuck, the gum only went up to her calf. Now when Fred is stuck with her, it comes all the way up to their knees! How does this affect Fred? Now he's preoccupied at work. He's thinking about having to come home and prepare meals. He wonders if Tammy is going to be drunk or sober. Will she embarrass him at the dinner party next week? He can't be as productive at work. He thinks more and more about her. He's not available to his kids on a consistent basis anymore. He's not always helping them with their homework. Fred is even beginning to drink with Tammy sometimes. So all of a sudden he's stuck.

"We then have the oldest child, Jimmy. Jimmy's very concerned because not only is Mom stuck, but Dad's stuck too. Neither parent is there for him on a consistent basis. Out of love and concern, he tries to help them get unstuck. As Jimmy tries to get his parents unstuck, look what happens. He also gets stuck in the gum. How does this affect Jimmy? His life isn't as free.

"How does this happen? Jimmy has a hard time concentrating in school. He thinks about having to go home to take care of a younger brother and sister. He's thinking about whether or not he should bring friends home. He might get embarrassed by what's happening there. He's real concerned. Jimmy doesn't have very many opportunities to play anymore because he's taking care of his younger brother and sister. When he does have a chance to play, he's often worried about Mom and Dad. He might be yelled at for something he didn't do.

"As younger brother and sister attempt to help Mom, Dad, and Jimmy get unstuck from the bubble gum, they will get stuck too. The entire family gets stuck. That's the Bubble Gum Family. Why do the kids get stuck? This is important. Why do kids get stuck in the bubble gum? They get stuck because they try to help their parents first. So if kids get stuck because they try to help, how do kids get unstuck? Kids get unstuck when they stop trying to take care of other people in the family, like Mom, Dad, brothers or sisters. They can begin to take good care of themselves. That's how kids get unstuck from the bubble gum.

"What does it mean to take care of yourself? In what different ways can kids take good care of themselves? Go out and play. Talk to a teacher. Ask a counselor for help. Go to a neighbor's house. Call Grandma if there's a mess at the house and you don't want to be there. These are some different ways kids can take care of themselves.

"Notice how everyone attempted to help Tammy. They were all around her. Everyone got stuck in the bubble gum. Even if she wanted to get unstuck, she couldn't! There was no room for her to get out. The family had blocked her path to recovery. Kids need to take care of themselves and not get stuck caring for others first.

"We have to remember that recovery takes time. There might be a time when Jimmy starts to take good care of himself and gets unstuck, but two weeks from now there will be a big dinner party at the house with Dad's business associates. Mom is still stuck in the bubble gum, so Jimmy might have to do all the preparations.

"Recovery is a process. We take two steps forward and because we're human, sometimes we take a step backward. So we get stuck and unstuck.

"I am thirty-two years old. When I was a teenager, I was so stuck in bubble gum that it came up to my neck. I have been in recovery for a long time now. I don't have bubble gum up to my neck anymore. I still have bubble gum, but now it's bubble gum from about the ankle down. That's why I stay in recovery to help me get off the rest of that bubble gum.

"That's the Bubble Gum Family."

This activity is taken from *Kids' Power: Healing Games for Children of Alcoholics*

Addiction Illustrated
(Ages 8 and up)

A good follow-up activity used with virtually any exercise in this section (especially with Bicycle or Letters to the Disease), Addiction Illustrated assists children in deepening their knowledge and understanding of the disease concept. Working in small groups to complete this task, youngsters not only learn from one another in a cooperative fashion but also further develop their socialization skills in the process.

DESCRIPTION

After one or two introductory exercises and subsequent discussions about family addiction and codependency, the facilitator puts youngsters in groups of three or more. Giving each group paper, a pencil, and magic markers, the facilitator challenges children to remember all they've learned about addiction and to use it in this activity. A brief follow-up session stressing key concepts can be helpful here. The facilitator then writes the word *addiction* vertically on a greaseboard, letter by letter. Youngsters are instructed to do the same on their group sheets.

The facilitator then asks each group to brainstorm describing this disease using a word or group of words starting with each letter in *addiction*. For example, the *a* could stand for "*a*lways thinking about the disease", one *d* could stand for "*d*enial," and so on using all the letters. By working in small groups children can learn from one another. The facilitator roams around the room and offers support, suggestions, and encouragement. Once completed, each group may share its creation with the larger group.

EXAMPLE

After concentrating on this activity for more than twenty-five minutes, Michael and Cassie both remarked that they understood addiction better by helping each other. "I guess it's really not my fault," Cassie shared in large group discussion. "I keep telling you that," chimed Mike. "Now I'm really beginning to believe it myself, too!"

AFFIRMATIONS

"It's okay to talk about family addiction with people who understand."

"All my feelings are okay."

"I can take good care of myself by sharing my problems and feelings with people I trust."

COMMENTS

You can repeat this activity using the word *codependency* if time allows. This also proves to be a powerful exercise.

With the children's permission, tape their creations to the group room's walls for future reference. These posters can serve as powerful visual reminders that addiction/codependency is not the children's fault and that they can't make it better.

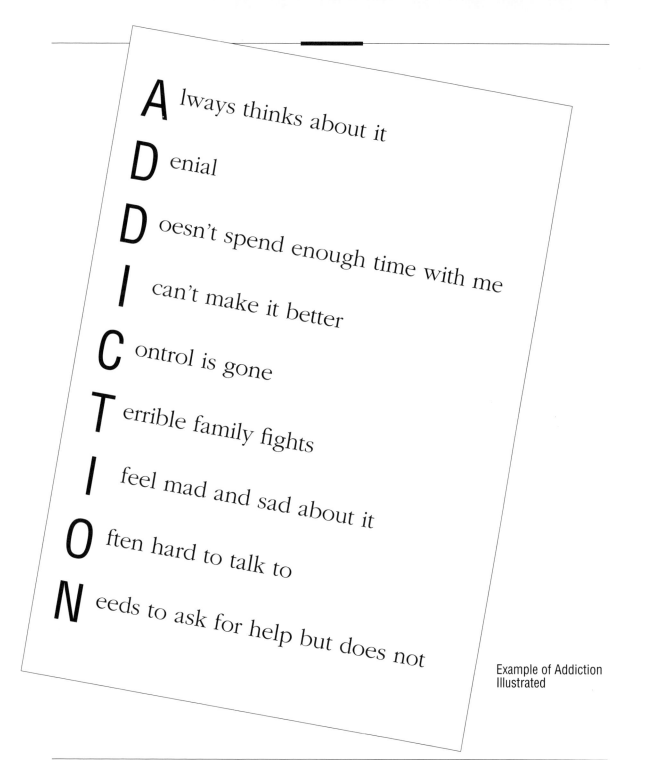

A lways thinks about it

D enial

D oesn't spend enough time with me

I can't make it better

C ontrol is gone

T errible family fights

I feel mad and sad about it

O ften hard to talk to

N eeds to ask for help but does not

Example of Addiction
Illustrated

Rad Ads
(Ages 7 and up)

This activity helps youngsters come to a deeper understanding about alcohol, other drugs, and addiction. Through their creativity and shared experiences, children describe a side of this powerful disease that rarely gets alluded to in any advertising. Along the way kids again realize that the disease is not their fault and that they are not alone.

DESCRIPTION

The facilitator tapes a variety of advertisements for alcohol and other drugs on the group room walls. Youngsters stroll around the room and closely scrutinize the ads, which stress the good life, beautiful people, fun, excitement, instant relief, and pleasure. A brief discussion takes place as youngsters comment on what they see in each ad, what the ad appears to be promising, and what makes it so appealing that people want to try the product.

Following this discussion, the facilitator asks the youngsters to think about what is missing from the various ads, specifically the negative side of alcohol and other drug addiction. Drawing largely from their own experiences, children then create advertisements about the perils of alcohol and other drug abuse and addiction. Youngsters draw scenes about parental fighting, family violence, broken promises, child abuse, and family members relapsing. Sometimes they draw pictures of people in hospitals, jails, or actually dying as a result of their addiction.

Youngsters have the option to share their pictures with the group. In reviewing these rad ads the facilitator stresses that addiction isn't the kids' fault and that they can't make it better, either. The ads help children see that they all have similar problems and feelings. They really are not alone.

EXAMPLE

Roberto's rad ad portrayed paramedics carrying a man on a stretcher and loading him into an ambulance. The caption above the picture read, "Be Smart, Don't Start." In sharing his creation with the group, Roberto described how his uncle died from using too much cocaine. His eyes filled with tears as he acknowledged his sadness. This was the first time in group that Roberto was able to talk about his uncle.

AFFIRMATIONS

"I can express all my feelings honestly."

"Lots of kids live with addiction problems in their families."

"I can share problems with people I trust."

COMMENTS

An optional follow up is to tape the rad ads on the walls to use for further reference in discussing the disease concept of addiction.

Encourage youngsters also to focus on other addictions in their ads, especially those that relate to their family experiences, such as food, tobacco, work, gambling, and relationship addictions.

An excellent follow up activity is Alphabet Soup Revisited.

MATERIALS
- Alcohol and other drug advertisements from magazines
- Paper
- Crayons, markers, and colored pencils

Example of Rad Ad

The Disease Game
(Ages 6 and up)

A visual exercise providing a different look at addiction, the Disease Game portrays how everyone in the family is impacted and affected. Even more important, this activity lets children see that no matter how hard they try or what they do they cannot make everything better. This game also demonstrates that youngsters have absolutely nothing to do with the genesis of the disease.

DESCRIPTION

The facilitator asks for a volunteer to role-play the addicted person. The volunteer sits in a chair in the front of the room and is completely covered by a blanket. The facilitator whispers in the volunteer's ear not to take the blanket off throughout the exercise. The facilitator explains to the group that the blanket represents the disease, especially how it covers the person that the youngsters love. The facilitator goes on to describe that the addict can't be present and emotionally available to take care of the kids in a consistent manner when he or she is consumed by the disease.

At the beginning of this activity, youngsters are asked what it feels like when their loved one is stuck and covered by the disease. This visual representation so graphically mirrors the disease that some youngsters immediately get in touch with anger, fear, hurt, sadness, loneliness, and shame. As they share that they'd like their loved one to be free of the addiction, youngsters come up one by one and try to get the addiction (namely, the blanket) off their loved one. Despite the children's begging, pleading, threatening, and physically struggling, the addict refuses to let go of the blanket. Sometimes during the course of the activity a youngster attempts to rip the blanket off the volunteer to stop the addiction (even though at the onset the one rule is that children may try anything except ripping off the blanket). If the child is indeed successful in ripping it off, the addict simply puts on another blanket, which the facilitator has available nearby. A discussion follows on how children can't make the addiction better, no matter what they try.

EXAMPLE

Cindy was getting nowhere fast trying to get off "Dad's blanket." This nine-year-old screamed, yelled, and threatened to run away, all to no avail. Finally, out of frustration, she ripped the blanket off, half-danced around the room, and smiled that she had made it better. Cindy was oblivious to the addict putting on another blanket. Once she noticed this, Cindy stopped in her tracks and yelled, "I hate this game. I don't wanna do this no more." With a little help she shared, "When Dad is sick, I feel angry, very angry."

AFFIRMATIONS

"It's okay to take good care of myself."

"I can love my parents and let go of their problems."

"I can learn that family addiction is not my responsibility."

Follow up this activity with Alphabet Soup Revisited (see Wednesday's activities). It reinforces the concepts in this game.

An important option here is to discuss that children didn't cause the addiction in the first place. It's not their fault.

MATERIALS
- Two blankets
- A chair

Bicycle II
(Ages 8 and up)

A powerful follow-up to Bicycle, this activity enables children to see how they have been impacted by addiction in their families. It also provides some clues about the necessity to care for themselves, because they can't stop the addiction or make it better.

DESCRIPTION

Bicycle provides a graphic visual of an addicted person speeding down the hill without brakes (the loss of control) and ultimately crashing. The facilitator introduces this visual to the group and asks if anyone has ever tried to stop "the crash." A discussion follows as the facilitator records the responses on newsprint or a greaseboard. Youngsters talk about hiding alcohol and other drugs, taking over parental responsibilities, attempting to resolve family conflicts, and holding in their feelings as ways to slow down and/or stop "the crash." Group members then share the anger, frustration, and guilt they feel upon discovering that these behaviors don't stop the addiction from progressing.

Going back to the visual in Bicycle, the facilitator role-plays an addict and climbs to the top of a hill. Ultimately, the addict will come speeding down the hill, without brakes, and crash, that is the process of addiction. The facilitator asks for a volunteer to role-play a child. The child stands across the room and puts his or her hands up, symbolizing an effort to stop the addicted parent and prevent the impending crash. As the rest of the group watches, the addict jogs across the room and crashes into the child who is attempting to make everything better. Bicycle II dramatically demonstrates how youngsters are impacted by addiction. The child and the rest of the group share feelings and thoughts about what they just observed and experienced. The facilitator weaves into the discussion suggestions of what the crash may represent—broken promises, getting yelled at, not getting to spend quality time with the parent, all the ways children get hurt by what is happening. After everyone has had the opportunity to role-play the child trying to stop the crash, the facilitator ends the activity by asking the group what they can do to take better care of themselves. A rich discussion follows.

EXAMPLE

Roberto volunteered to role-play the child trying to prevent the addict's crash four times during group. Convinced he could make everything better, this ten-year-old kept standing there and ultimately getting slammed by the addict speeding out of control. Each time he asked for another turn, only to get run into again. Finally his eyes filled with tears and he blurted out, "I'm sad. I don't know what to do." The group rang out, "Get out of the way, Roberto. Take care of yourself." Somewhat skeptical, Roberto decided to give it another try. This time, Roberto stepped aside and avoided the crash.

AFFIRMATIONS

"It's important to take good care of myself."

"I deserve to be safe."

"I can let others take care of their own problems."

COMMENTS As each child volunteers to stop the addict's out of control spiral, the facilitator role-playing the addict can use a different addiction, alcohol, other drugs, work, gambling, etc.. This variety adds to the depth and richness of the experience.

It often works to do Bicycle during one session and then Bicycle II as a follow-up the next session.

MATERIALS
- Bicycle Ride Narrative
- Colored markers
- Newsprint or greaseboard

Treatment-n-Recovery
(Ages 6 and up)

A logical extension of the Addiction Game, this visual and kinesthetic activity helps children gain a new and deeper understanding of treatment and the recovery process. Youngsters also come to see that they are not responsible for their parents' recovery, but that they are responsible for taking care of themselves.

DESCRIPTION

In the Addiction Game, the dependent eventually gets hooked by the disease of addiction (role-played by the facilitator). The disease grabs the person by the arms and won't let him or her go, thus symbolizing how that person has been hooked, trapped, and consumed by addiction. After a brief discussion about how addiction now runs that individual's life, youngsters try different ways to get the person unstuck, all to no avail. Group members not only see that the addiction is not their fault, but also that they can't make everything better. This is the essence of the Addiction Game.

But how do people get better from addiction? While the disease still firmly has a grasp on the dependent, the group brainstorms ways in which the person can get better. When someone yells that the addicted person needs to ask for and get help, the dependent yells out, "Help. I need help. Please help." Role-playing Treatment-n-Recovery, the other facilitator makes his or her way to the person asking for help. When Treatment-n-Recovery gets close, the disease runs away out of fear. Treatment-n-Recovery introduces itself to the dependent and shares how it can help. "I'll help you learn to love yourself, be honest, share feelings, and learn how to take care of yourself and be free." The dependent learns that Treatment-n-Recovery only stays around if the person really wants to get better. Treatment-n-Recovery demonstrates that it is a safety net that protects the person from alcohol, other drugs, or whatever the person is hooked on. The disease lurks on the other side of the room, waiting to pounce on the dependent, but it can't do so while Treatment-n-Recovery is around.

All group members get the opportunity to role-play the dependent and ask Treatment-n-Recovery for help. A discussion follows on all the things that comprise Treatment-n-Recovery: treatment, aftercare, counseling, and Twelve-Step meetings like AA, NA, Al-Anon, etc..

EXAMPLE

Cathey yelled for help and was quickly met by Treatment-n-Recovery. At first, this six-year-old stood behind Treatment-n-Recovery for support and protection. With the disease lurking across the room and Cathey feeling safer, she came out from behind Treatment-n-Recovery and started taunting the disease. "You'll never get me again, you big creep," she boasted amidst the giggles and laughter of the group. Growing braver by the second, Cathey moved toward the disease as it whispered softly, "Come and say it right to me." Leaving Treatment-n-Recovery, Cathey got close to the disease to utter those same words when she got hooked by it again. The facilitators briefly stopped the game and asked the group what had happened. Bertha yelled out, "She got hooked again. That's relapse. You leave Treatment-n-Recovery and you can have a relapse." What insight for this bright child!

AFFIRMATIONS

"It's okay to ask for help."

"There are safe people and places to turn to for help."

COMMENTS

Emphasize that relapse also is not the child's fault. It occurs because the addicted person doesn't stay with Treatment-n-Recovery.

During each child's role-play pick a different process or substance, such as alcohol, cocaine, pain medication, other drugs, food, work, exercise, gambling or shopping for them to be hooked on. This adds depth and richness to the experience.

If your group has only one facilitator, pick a child to play Treatment-n-Recovery.

Rock-n-Roll Recovery
(Ages 10 and up)

Rock-n-Roll Recovery combines youngsters' affinity for rock and rap songs, their experiences and feelings living in high-stress families, and their inherent creativity to deepen their understanding of addiction, codependency, and related problems. This activity is a living manifestation of the old adage, Learning by Doing.

DESCRIPTION

Music is a universal language that can deeply touch the soul. The facilitator introduces the group to popular rap or rock melodies by playing the songs on a boom box. After giving the participants a copy of the various lyrics, the facilitator divides the members into two small groups and asks each, with the facilitator's support and guidance, to pick one song on which to focus. The task of each group is to rewrite the song's lyrics to describe the children's experiences living with addiction, as well as their pursuits of recovery. This project can be completed over the course of two to four sessions. It requires considerable dialogue, debate, and incorporation of the many new concepts youngsters are learning in group. For example, three twelve-year-olds and their facilitator rewrote the lyrics of Elton John's song, "I Guess That's Why They Call It The Blues," over a course of three sessions. Through much talking, feeling, trusting, and cooperating, the group created, "I Guess That's Why I'm Always Confused," a powerful song that succinctly describes living in an addicted family. Much healing took place along the way (lyrics to "I Guess That's Why I'm Always Confused" can be found following this exercise).

EXAMPLE

Four eleven-year-olds and their facilitator rewrote the lyrics of Janet Jackson's "What Have You Done for Me Lately?" over the course of five sessions. "Why Don't You Treat Yourself Greatly" is a song that describes a variety of self-care strategies children can employ on a daily basis. Amanda shared that she sings the song anytime things start going bad for her. "The melody gets in my head and I sing the words. It reminds me to take good care of myself."

AFFIRMATIONS

"I am a beautiful and creative person."

"I have special qualities. I can contribute them to the group."

COMMENTS

It is important to choose rap and rock melodies that have a very good beat. Be sure to pick songs with healthy lyrics.

Help the group get started with a theme or concept, then get out of the way so the kids can do the work. The kids will let you know if they need assistance.

MATERIALS
- Boom box
- Cassette tapes of popular songs and their lyrics
- Paper
- Pencils

"I Guess That's Why I'm Always Confused"

Just wish it away
Don't look at it
Pretend it's all better
My parents can't stop
I can honestly say they just never get better
Booze and drugs always stay
To cast their demons inside
And it won't be long before Mom and Dad go to their crazy place
It's time to hide

And I guess that's why I'm always confused
Scared, all alone, and verbally abused
Parents are children
Fighting not hugging
Exploding like thunder
Under their drugging
I guess that's why I'm always confused

Just stare into space
I've been disgraced
Friends just don't understand
Live for each second
With pained reservations and
Never count on parents' plans
It's just no use
Cry in the night if it helps
Yet nothing helps
It seems they love booze
More than they love me or life itself

I guess that's why I'm always confused
Scared, all alone, and verbally abused
Parents are children
Fighting not hugging
Exploding like thunder
Under their drugging
And I guess that's why I'm always confused

(sung to "I Guess That's Why They Call It The Blues" by Elton John)

High-Risk Me
(Ages 6 and up)

A sculpture that clearly portrays the multigenerational family legacy of addiction, High-Risk Me assists youngsters in understanding that they have a greater chance to carry on addictive behaviors. Without preaching, lecturing, or using scare tactics this activity illustrates how addiction and codependency get passed on and points out the necessity for children to develop healthy living skills as a preventative mechanism.

DESCRIPTION

Because this sculpture involves every member of the group, all youngsters are up and moving as they actively participate in this process. The facilitator adjusts the various roles in the sculpture based on the number of youngsters in group. At a minimum the roles must include a star, a couple of feelings, a couple of addictions, and a counselor to offer helpful suggestions after the sculpture is complete.

The facilitator picks children to play the various parts and gives each one a yellow self-stick note that delineates his or her role. Beginning with the star the facilitator describes how this person grew up in a family where no one openly shared their emotions so the star never learned the important skill of identifying and expressing feelings. Instead, this person has learned to stuff his or her feelings. One by one the youngsters who are role-playing feelings come forward, anger, sadness, fear, and hurt. As each feeling introduces itself to the star, the feeling grabs hold of this person, representing how the feeling gets stuffed. Soon the star is stuck in his or her feelings, as each one grabs and holds on to the person. In this manner, the children are creating a human sculpture. The star describes how stuck and fatigued he or she becomes as a result of carrying around stuffed feelings all day.

Next alcohol and/or other drugs are introduced to the star. For a short period the chemicals put the feelings to sleep and the star appears to be unstuck and free. As this person's relationship with the chemicals gets closer and closer, alcohol and other drugs soon hook the star. This is addiction in action. Gradually the chemicals stop working and the person is not only hooked to chemicals but also still carries around the baggage of stuffed feelings. The counselor is now called in to offer insight about recovery, first to put the addictions aside and then to teach the person how to express feelings in a healthy way.

A discussion follows on what a youngster can learn growing up in such a family, how to stuff feelings; how to turn to alcohol, other drugs, and other substances and processes as a means of coping with uncomfortable feelings and problems; and how to look for answers outside of the self. A connection is made about how a child learning such messages in the family increases his or her risk of developing similar problems.

EXAMPLE

Candace, an exuberant yet confused eleven-year-old, focused intently on every aspect of the sculpture. During the discussion she chimed in, "Now I really understand what my father is going through. I gotta take better care of myself by sharing my feelings with people I trust." A quiet confidence came over Candace as her understanding of addiction and recovery was deepened through this visual, kinesthetic exercise.

AFFIRMATIONS

"All my feelings are okay."

"I can express my feelings honestly."

"I can learn new tools and skills to take good care of myself."

"I can have recovery just for myself."

COMMENTS

This activity is a good one to use for closure on this theme, because youngsters respond favorably to it, and it also often ties up any loose ends about understanding addiction.

If time permits add addictions to food, work, raging, smoking, and gambling to the sculpture to help children see how one addiction may be substituted for another.

Emphasize the recovery process for everyone, especially children, and how it involves the open and honest expression of feelings.

MATERIALS

- Self-stick notes
- Markers

Can't Cure It Game
(Ages 6 and up)

A spin-off of the Disease Game, this visual activity helps children to understand that they are not responsible for a loved one's relapse. On a larger scale, youngsters may realize that a loved one's recovery isn't their responsibility, as kids can't control or cure family addiction and codependency. At the same time, children are encouraged to take good care of themselves.

DESCRIPTION

The facilitator reviews the concepts of the Disease Game with the only difference being that this person plays the dependent. Sitting in a chair wrapped in a blanket of addiction, the facilitator makes the choice to seek recovery and takes off the blanket in the process. A discussion ensues about the realities of recovery as the facilitator pins the blanket to the wall behind his or her chair. Although the dependent is much more present and emotionally available, the disease still looms large in the background. This visual representation assists youngsters in getting in touch with their fears of relapse.

The facilitator now asks youngsters to ponder the worst thing they could do or say to the dependent. One by one the children approach the dependent and talk about school suspensions, getting in trouble with the police, and hurling such comments as "I hate you" or "I wish you were dead." The dependent listens to each comment, takes a deep breath, and tells each boy or girl, "The decision to drink, use, or rage again is completely mine. Nothing you could ever say or do can make me relapse, except me." Even though the dependent may grab at the blanket and become wrapped in it again, the facilitator repeats, "If I should ever relapse it's completely up to me, it's not your fault; you can never control or cure my problems or my disease." A follow-up discussion reinforces these major messages.

EXAMPLE

Jacki yelled in anger and resentment at the dependent for past indiscretions. "You've never been a real dad to me. I hate you, just go away." Upon hearing this verbal barrage the dependent reassured Jacki, "My disease and recovery belong to me. If I relapse I will be solely responsible for it." Jacki sat back down and was quiet for a long time as she watched other kids go though this same process. At its conclusion Jacki beamed, "It's really not me. It's really not me," and a huge smile covered her face.

AFFIRMATIONS

"I can take good care of myself."

"I can learn about addiction, it's not my fault; I can't control it or cure it."

"I am a beautiful and special person."

COMMENTS

Use this activity after youngsters have digested the message of the Disease Game.

Repeating this activity twice during the week sometimes helps to reinforce the major messages here.

MATERIALS
- Chair
- Blanket
- Pushpins

Dear Gabby
(Ages 4 and up)

This light, fun-filled exercise serves as a final course in strengthening youngsters' understanding of the disease concept of addiction and codependency. By presenting a steady stream of erroneous yet largely held beliefs about this illness, the facilitator challenges group members to collectively apply all the new information they've gleaned about this highly misunderstood phenomenon. Kids not only learn from one another but also have fun in the process.

DESCRIPTION

After completing a few other games and activities with this theme, the facilitator informs the group that a guest expert will be joining them later in the day to offer new insight and information on addiction and codependency. Youngsters write a variety of questions on this topic for the expert to answer. After a break in the children's program, the facilitator enters the room dressed in a colorful wig and outrageous costume. The facilitator introduces himself or herself as "Dear Gabby," an expert in these issues. Gabby reads the children's questions and proceeds to give long-winded, incorrect answers, such as "it really is the kids' fault that parents have addiction and codependency problems," or "it's the children's job to take good care of their parents."

A discussion follows where the real experts, the children, set Gabby straight about addiction and codependency. The group reviews the major concepts.

EXAMPLE

Bobbi Jo, usually quiet and reserved in group, became actively involved in the Dear Gabby exercise. The more Gabby went on about how addiction was all the kids' fault and how they could make it all better if they tried hard enough, the more vocal this nine-year-old became. Her arm shot in the air and as she was acknowledged, Bobbi Jo blurted out, "Addiction is a disease, it's no one's fault. Kids gotta take care of themselves. It's the only thing they can really do." Others responded with "Yeahs" or nodded their heads affirmatively. They were beginning to understand on a deeper level.

AFFIRMATIONS

"I can learn about addiction and codependency."

"It's okay to speak up for myself."

"I can learn to take good care of myself."

COMMENTS

Most youngsters giggle and laugh at Gabby's outrageous dress and totally inaccurate answers. They easily refute these responses and provide accurate information they've learned. Consequently, this game serves as an excellent final activity in this theme.

Combining this exercise with Alphabet Soup Revisited reinforces most of the key concepts presented here. (See Chapter 8 for this activity.)

Debrief with youngsters after this activity; tell them that you were trying to trick them and that it simply didn't work. Youngsters delight in the fact that the facilitator was unsuccessful in the effort.

MATERIALS
- Index cards
- Pencils
- Wig
- Outrageous dress (clothes that don't match in colors, two different socks, etc.)

Stuck in the Feelings Redux
(Ages 8 and up)

This visual and kinesthetic activity helps children make a connection between stuffed feelings and addiction. It clearly demonstrates the best way to deal with feelings, share them in balanced ways with safe people.

DESCRIPTION

This game begins right in the middle of Stuck in the Feelings (see Tuesday activities). The star has decided to keep all of his or her feelings inside and now must drag around the three youngsters who are role-playing different feelings. In only a few seconds the star feels weighed down by carrying around feelings. This person needs some quick relief but doesn't necessarily know what to do. Now the stage is set.

The facilitator, role-playing alcohol and other drugs (chemicals), walks up to the star and offers help. "You look stuck and pressured but I can help you get free. All you gotta do is drink enough of me and you'll be unstuck." Convincing the star to at least give them a try, chemicals give the stuck person a couple of drinks. Then chemicals put all the stuck feelings to sleep, with a wave of a hand each feeling closes his or her eyes. The star is free for awhile and doesn't feel the pressure and weight of carrying around all those feelings. The star sees the power that alcohol and other drugs seem to possess. Yet when chemicals finally leave, the feelings wake up now more refreshed and stronger. Often another feeling (again, a child role-playing it) joins the others, such as guilt or embarrassment, in response to the star's behavior when using the chemicals. Ultimately, the star is even more stuck and might look to chemicals to get free again, even though it would be only temporary. This vicious cycle can continue to escalate. The game proceeds until everyone has had a chance to play the star. A discussion follows on how addiction often is connected to stuck and painful feelings. The facilitator emphasizes that the best way to deal with stuffed feelings is to share them with safe people, those you can truly trust.

EXAMPLE

Although initially reluctant to do so, Louisa took the alcohol and finally got free. She ran and skipped around the room with her new found feelings, "Ha, ha, ha. You'll never trap me again." But soon alcohol left, and the feelings woke up and grabbed the eight-year-old all over again. Much to her surprise, guilt introduced itself to Louisa and grabbed onto her as well. "I'm not doing this again. It only gets worse," she blurted out. The group responded with clapping and cheering.

AFFIRMATIONS

"It's important to take good care of myself."

"I can share my feelings with people I trust."

When each child takes a turn being the star, the facilitator can use a different substance or process to momentarily free the feelings, such as cocaine, smoking, food, work, gambling, relationships, etc..

During the follow-up discussion, the facilitator can emphasize that sharing feelings is the best way to take care of oneself, yet sometimes it is important to hold feelings until the child finds a safe person with whom to talk.

An option here is to help children make the connection between depression and stuffed feelings.

High-Risk Me, Too
(Ages 6 and up)

A visual activity combining fun with learning, High-Risk Me, Too teaches youngsters about various risk factors for alcoholism and other drug addiction. This game also empowers children to make healthy choices when it comes to using alcohol and other drugs, especially in terms of reducing their own risk factors.

DESCRIPTION

The facilitator instructs the children to sit in a large circle with plenty of room between group members to create lots of space inside the circle. The facilitator passes out six small Velcro® balls and tells the group that the balls symbolize alcohol and other drugs. The kids gently toss the chemical balls back and forth. Once they get the hang of it, the facilitator stops the process so the game can begin. The facilitator explains that he or she will role-play many different people and walk through the valley of alcohol and other drugs as the children toss the chemicals. If a chemical ball sticks to the person, it represents addiction, being hooked.

First the facilitator plays a twenty-five-year-old with no family history of addiction. This person walks through the valley twice and then yells, "I've had enough," and leaves. While it's possible for a Velcro ball to stick here, it very rarely happens, especially to a person who doesn't spend much time in the valley. Next the facilitator plays a sixteen-year-old with no family history of addiction. Because the sixteen-year-old has a greater risk, the facilitator tapes a 2″ x 4″ foam target on his or her stomach. Walking through the valley of chemicals, the person has a greater chance of getting hooked. The longer the person stays in the valley, the more likely addiction becomes.

Now the facilitator plays a sixteen-year-old with addiction problems on one side of the family. Here the person wears a 4″ x 6″ foam target. (A hole is punched through the top of the foam and a long piece of yarn is put through and tied in a knot so that the target can be worn, see illustration.) This person is at even greater risk of getting hooked, even if he or she spends less time in the valley. Yet sometimes this person spends extra time there and never gets hooked by the chemicals. Still that person has a greater risk. Last, the facilitator becomes a sixteen-year-old with a history of addiction on both sides of the family. This individual wears two 4″ x 6″ targets, one in front and one in back. Walking through the valley, this person is an even bigger target, although it's still possible to not get hooked. Now group members take turns role-playing various people and trying to go in the valley without getting hooked. A follow-up discussion ensues about risk factors and what youngsters can do to lessen their risks. (See example).

EXAMPLE

Clint put on two foam targets to depict the alcoholism on both sides of his family. After running, stopping, twisting, turning, falling, and jumping to avoid the chemicals from hooking him, he quickly bolted out of the valley. "I'm not going anywhere near that place," Clint stated with the wisdom of his nine years. The group had been given a new option, staying away from chemicals. The children discussed how this was the best choice of all.

AFFIRMATIONS

"I can make healthy choices to take care of myself."

"I can say no to alcohol and other drugs. I can say yes to life."

COMMENTS

Especially with younger children, make sure they softly toss the Velcro balls, as they can get very excited in their zeal to get the person hooked.

Introduce the choice of not walking through the valley of chemicals if group members don't come up with it themselves.

MATERIALS

- Six small Velcro balls
- One 2″ x 4″ foam target with masking tape
- Two 4″ x 6″ foam targets with yarn tied through each

Example of velcro balls
on foam target

73]

Tough Love Lists
(Ages 8 and up)

After coming to a better understanding of addiction, codependency, depression, and other mental health concerns, youngsters are prepared to complete a tough love list for the family member who is a patient. Typically done early Monday afternoon, the list allows children to honestly confront their loved one's behaviors and openly share feelings in the process. For many this marks the first time youngsters have talked about the "family secrets" and honestly expressed their feelings in a direct way. Because children have learned to survive their inconsistent and unpredictable environments by not talking, trusting, and feeling, they may be resistant or afraid to prepare and present this list.

DESCRIPTION

The facilitator begins the process by asking group members to think about the problems present in their families, fighting, broken promises, drinking, drugging, yelling, parents not listening or never around are but a few examples. Using newsprint or a greaseboard, the facilitator lists all the children's responses under the category heading of Problems. Once completed, a similar process takes place as the youngsters brainstorm feelings they experience when contending with such problems. Again the facilitator writes their responses under the Feelings category. Children are then introduced to the "When you — I feel" format as the facilitator explains how this method of confrontation works: When you (state the problem behavior), I feel (describe the feeling or feelings). The facilitator gives the group a few examples to clearly illustrate the format: "Dad, when you fight with Mom I feel angry, scared, and sad"; or "Mom, when you sit around the house all day and cry I feel guilty and sad."

After a brief discussion the facilitator gives the group members tough love lists to complete (see next page). Roaming around the room from youngster to youngster the facilitator provides support, encouragement, and assistance. When everyone finishes his or her list the facilitator leads the group through a role-play so children can see how the list sharing takes place and can practice giving their lists if they so desire. Sometimes the facilitator will actually accompany a child to family group to support the child in presenting the tough love list.

MATERIALS

- Newsprint or greaseboard
- Tough Love Lists

TOUGH LOVE LISTS

My Feelings List For:

When you—   I feel—

_____   _____

_____   _____

_____   _____

_____   _____

When you—   I feel—

_____   _____

_____   _____

_____   _____

_____   _____

When you—   I feel—

_____   _____

_____   _____

_____   _____

_____   _____

When you—   I feel—

_____   _____

_____   _____

_____   _____

_____   _____

Tuesday

All My Feelings Are Okay — Feelings

KEY CONCEPTS
- All my feelings are okay.
- Some feelings are more difficult to express than others.
- There are safe people I can talk to about my feelings.

GOALS
- To help children identify, express, and own their feelings.
- To assist children in understanding the difference between comfortable and uncomfortable feelings.
- To guide children in determining who are safe people with whom to share feelings and get support.
- To learn a variety of healthy ways to cope with feelings.

ACTIVITIES

A Brainstorm of Feelings

Feelings Alphabet

Frozen Feelings Game

Stuffed Problems and Feelings

Feeling Puppet Family

Guess My Feeling Game

Stuck in the Feelings Game

Feelings Mate

Feelings Wheel

A Bag o' Feelings

Artwork

The Feelings Place

Feelings Face Case

Our Common Bond, Feelings

Share 'em or Stuff 'em Game

BOOKS/STORIES	"Fuzzy's Feelings" (In *An Elephant in the Living Room*)
	"Ms. Piggy's Secret" (In *Kids Are Special* curriculum)
	Pepper
	The Happy Girl
FILMS:	*A Story About Feelings*
	Twee, Fiddle, and Huff
	All Bottled Up
SONGS	"Inside" by Jim Newton (*Friends of the Family* cassette)
	"The Frog Song" by Jim Newton (*Friends of the Family* cassette)
	"Understand" by Jim Newton (*Children at Heart* cassette)
	"I Believe You" by Peter Alsop (*Wake-Up* cassette)
	"Bored, Bored, Bored " by Peter Alsop (*Wha' D' Ya Wanna Do* cassette)
	"What if..." by Peter Alsop (*Pluggin' Away* cassette)

DAILY THEME

Mini-Lecture

Many youngsters lack the necessary vocabulary to identify and express their feelings. They tend to lump all feelings into good/bad or happy/sad categories. Children from addictive and codependent family systems become adept at covering up their feelings as a means of survival. When feelings are not openly and honestly expressed, youngsters learn to stuff their feelings inside, especially uncomfortable ones that are not acceptable to communicate in their families (such as being angry). This powerful "don't talk and don't feel" rule can be a pervasively entrenched message. Because emotions are not openly discussed, youngsters not only lack the opportunity for validation but also get cut off from fully experiencing those feelings and learning healthy ways to cope with them.

Help children understand that feelings are like road signs, signals to pay close attention to, and keep them safe on their journey. Have them imagine what it would be like if drivers didn't observe road signs. People would get lost, confused, and put themselves in potential danger. Like following road signs, paying attention to feelings helps keep people on the right path, safe and sure about where they are going.

Ask youngsters to brainstorm a variety of feelings on newsprint or a greaseboard. Explain how these emotions are among the many different ones humans experience on a daily basis. Moreover, explain that feelings are neither good nor bad, they just are. All feelings are okay; they are guideposts that signal people to take care of themselves. Differentiate between comfortable and uncomfortable feelings, and how expressing the latter sometimes can be quite difficult. Even so, all feelings are nevertheless normal and okay.

An option here is to introduce the concept of safe people (a concept that also gets attention on Wednesday, Taking Care of Me). Often the key to dealing with feelings is finding new tools to cope with them in balanced, safe, and healthy ways. By giving children maps of what makes certain people safe, youngsters can search out such people with whom to share their feelings. Give kids other options to express their feelings without hurting themselves or others, like scribbling a picture, writing a letter, running as fast as they can, or pounding on a pillow instead of a person when they feel angry.

In a nutshell, feelings are friends that guide youngsters on their way. All feelings are normal and okay. Assist youngsters in identifying, owning, and expressing their feelings in healthy ways (including talking about them with safe people).

A Brainstorm of Feelings
(Ages 6 and up)

This activity introduces youngsters to a wide range of feeling words. By developing an awareness that feelings are signs that guide one's journey, children come to realize that it is okay and normal to experience a large variety of emotions. This exercise empowers kids to identify and express feelings in new, healthy ways.

DESCRIPTION

On a greaseboard or newsprint, the group facilitator writes as many feeling words as the children can brainstorm. Challenging the group to come up with a reasonable list, such as twenty-five feeling words, can be fun. Sometimes it may become necessary to give youngsters a clue, such as "What feeling do you get when you are about to open your birthday presents?" (excited), or "How do you feel when you don't understand the math problem on the board at school?" (confused). Offering a challenge to the group helps them work together, which can encourage trust and bonding. The facilitator gives clues in an effort to create a balanced list of comfortable and uncomfortable feelings. An option is to let an older group member do the actual writing as others share feeling words.

Next the facilitator asks the children to count all the "bad" feelings on the brainstormed list. After they come up with a number, the facilitator explains that this was a trick question, as there are no bad feelings. All feelings are okay, and humans experience a wide range of them every day. The facilitator concludes this activity by explaining the differences between comfortable and uncomfortable feelings. Group discussion follows.

EXAMPLE

Willie looked perplexed when the group leader shared that all feelings are normal and okay. This eleven-year-old remained stuck to the notion that many feelings are bad. When the facilitator gently asked him what he was feeling, Willie quickly blurted, "I'm confused." With some discussion Willie realized that it was okay to feel confused, that it wasn't bad. Quickly his eyes lit up and a large grin crossed his face as Willie shared, "Oh, yeah, my feelings are okay!"

AFFIRMATIONS

"There are safe people I can talk to about my feelings."

"All my feelings are okay."

COMMENTS

This activity is a good introduction to the topic of feelings. Several of the following activities work extremely well in conjunction with it.

An option for younger children is to draw feeling faces instead of listing feeling words so that they may more actively participate in this exercise.

- Newsprint or greaseboard
- Markers

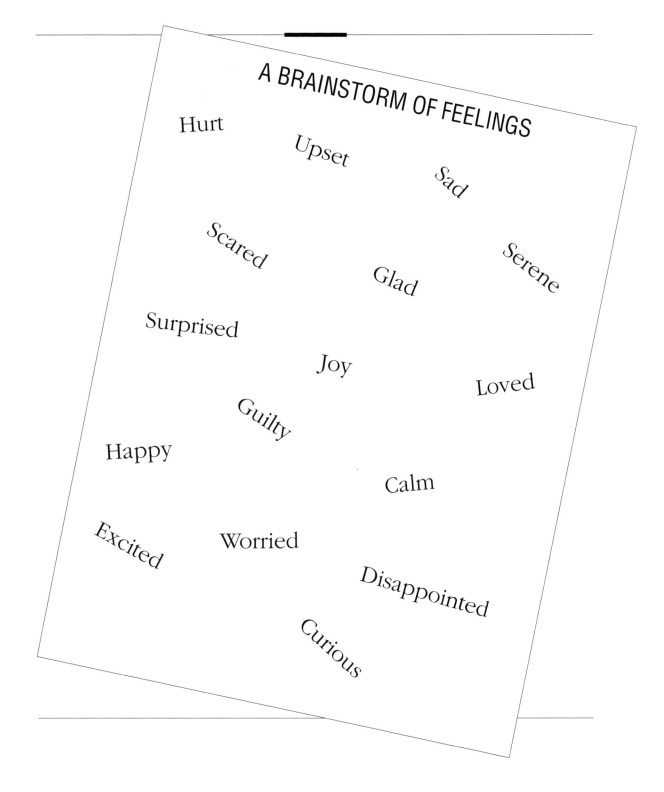

A BRAINSTORM OF FEELINGS

Hurt

Upset

Sad

Scared

Serene

Glad

Surprised

Joy

Loved

Guilty

Happy

Calm

Excited

Worried

Disappointed

Curious

Feelings Alphabet
(Ages 8 and up)

This game introduces kids to a wide range of feeling words, helps them to realize all feelings are okay, and lends itself to a discussion of safe and healthy ways to express feelings. The fun centers around youngsters trying to brainstorm feeling words for the letters x, y, *and* z *to successfully complete this activity.*

DESCRIPTION

Using newsprint or a greaseboard to write on, the group facilitator or a specially chosen youngster is the recorder for this activity. The object of the game is to come up with at least two feelings for every letter in the alphabet. The recorder begins by writing a big *A* and the members brainstorm two feelings that begin with that letter, such as angry and afraid. As the group weaves its way through the alphabet, the facilitator gives youngsters clues as they ask for help: for example, "What is the opposite of happy? Hint: it begins with a *U* (unhappy)." The facilitator assists the group and is particularly generous when it comes to feeling words beginning with *x, y,* and *z,* as xcited and xhausted will certainly suffice for the purpose of this exercise.

When this task is completed, the facilitator instructs the youngsters to count up all the "bad" feelings. As they come up with a number in their heads, the facilitator explains that this was really a trick, as there are no bad feelings. A discussion ensues about how all feelings are okay, and that people experience a wide range of them every day. The discussion is completed with an explanation of the differences between comfortable and uncomfortable feelings.

EXAMPLE

Tabitha eagerly looked around the room as other children raised their hands to acknowledge they had felt angry, bored, calm, dumb, and excited at some time in their lives. When it was her turn to share, Tabitha replied, "I thought I was the only kid who ever felt like that." As the children nodded their heads Tabitha sighed, looking relieved in finally understanding that she wasn't alone.

AFFIRMATIONS

"It's okay to talk about my feelings."

"All my feelings are okay."

COMMENTS

This activity is often easier for younger children than A Brainstorm of Feelings, because the alphabet letters *(A,* then *B,* then *C)* keep them focused on the task at hand.

Remember to celebrate the group's accomplishment of making it through the alphabet with feeling words.

MATERIALS

- Newsprint or greaseboard
- Markers

FEELINGS ALPHABET SAMPLE LIST

A Afraid, Angry, Anxious

B Bored, Brave

C Calm, Confused, Curious

D Different, Dumb, Disappointed

E Excited, Embarrassed

F Funny, Frightened

G Guilty, Glad

H Happy, Hopeless, Hurt

I Ignored, Important

J Joy, Jealous, Jumpy

K Kind, Karing

L Lonely, Love

M Mad, Mean, Mixed up

N Nice, Nerdy

O Overwhelmed, Outrageous

P Proud, Playful

Q Quiet, Queasy

R Rad, Restless

S Sad, Scared, Shame, Surprised

T Tired, Terrible

U Unloved, Uncomfortable

V Vicious, Violent

W Warm, Worried

X Xcited, Xhausted

Y Yucky, Yellow

Z Zany, Zippy

Frozen Feelings Game
(Ages 6 and up)

Children especially enjoy playing this game, which offers them choices about holding on to their feelings or sharing them with others. Youngsters learn about a variety of factors and conditions that make sharing feelings safe. Above all, kids come to realize that their feelings ultimately belong to them.

DESCRIPTION

This activity is best done in an open space where children can sit comfortably on the floor. After a brief discussion about how people either share or hold their feelings, the game begins. The facilitator places small index cards face down on the middle of the floor. Each card has one basic feeling written on it, such as angry, happy, sad, glad, scared, excited, surprised, afraid, or hurt. A volunteer picks a card and silently reads the feeling on it without letting anyone else see it. The facilitator instructs the youngster to sit anywhere in the room and hold on to that feeling so tightly that it becomes "frozen." The facilitator then tells the child that he or she has a choice to share or hold that particular feeling.

Group members share words of encouragement and affirmations, such as "All feelings are okay," "I'll listen if you'd like to talk," or "I'm a safe person to talk to," all in an attempt to assist the volunteer in "thawing" and sharing the feeling. The facilitator may chime in with, "What do you need to feel safe so you can share your feeling?" After a few minutes the youngster may decide to keep the feeling, or to share it and describe one time he or she actually felt that way. Repeat the game until everyone who would like a turn gets one.

Follow up with a discussion about the choices children have with their feelings and the conditions that provide the safety to share them.

EXAMPLE

LaShunda kept her head down and clutched her feeling card tightly. Her peers whispered softly, "Tell us your feeling, c'mon tell us," but got virtually no response as this nine-year-old remained frozen. Finally, she was awakened by these words from her best friend: "I care about you so don't keep it inside." LaShunda looked up with tears streaming down her face and said, "Sad, I feel sad when Dad smokes cocaine and never comes home."

AFFIRMATIONS

"My feelings belong to me."

"I can choose to share my feelings or to hold them."

COMMENTS

Don't make a value judgment about whether children share or keep their feelings. Empower them in understanding the choice is theirs.

Help youngsters determine when they can safely share their feelings.

MATERIALS

• Index cards with a feeling written on each one

Stuffed Problems and Feelings
(Ages 6 and up)

This experiential exercise helps children to kinesthetically understand the consequences of holding problems and feelings inside. In a fun way, it also introduces them to the recovery process of identifying problems and expressing feelings. Youngsters actually experience freedom by initiating this process for themselves.

DESCRIPTION

With the children sitting in a circle, the group facilitator places a tote bag in the middle. Unbeknownst to the kids the bag is full of brightly colored rocks, each with a problem (such as addiction, depression, codependency, and family secrets) or a feeling (such as anger, scared, hurt, shame, guilty, and sad) painted on it. The facilitator describes how everyone who comes to Sierra Tucson has been carrying around such a bag inside. One by one youngsters pick up the bag and attempt to walk around the room carrying it. The facilitator asks such questions as, "How does it feel carrying all this stuff?", "When you carry such a heavy load what are you always thinking about?", and "Can you be free to be a kid and laugh and play when you've always got that bag with you?"

After a brief discussion, the bag is returned to the middle of the circle and the facilitator opens it up and explores its contents. One by one the children reach into the bag, take out a rock, and read the problem or feeling on it. When the addiction rock comes out the facilitator asks how many kids have addiction problems in their families. Many hands are raised. The facilitator acknowledges the children and states, "We'll learn lots about addiction this week, especially that it's not the kids' fault." When a feeling rock gets pulled out the facilitator asks how many children have felt this way, and kids have a chance to share feelings. Before long the bag is empty and everyone has the chance to carry it around again. All are amazed at how much lighter the bag is because they talked about their problems and feelings.

EXAMPLE

Jordan, age 6, could barely lift the full bag off the floor and had to drag it across the room. He especially enjoyed how much lighter it felt after the sharing session. At the end of the discussion he uttered, "I want to get rid of some rocks about Mom's divorce. I feel sad and scared."

AFFIRMATIONS

"I can share my problems and feelings with people who care."

"All my feelings are okay."

COMMENTS

This is an excellent introductory activity to get the group rolling.

As youngsters share problems and express feelings during the week, celebrate their progress by acknowledging "you let go of a couple more rocks today. Hooray!"

MATERIALS   • Tote bag

• Ten rocks, each painted with an individual feeling or problem

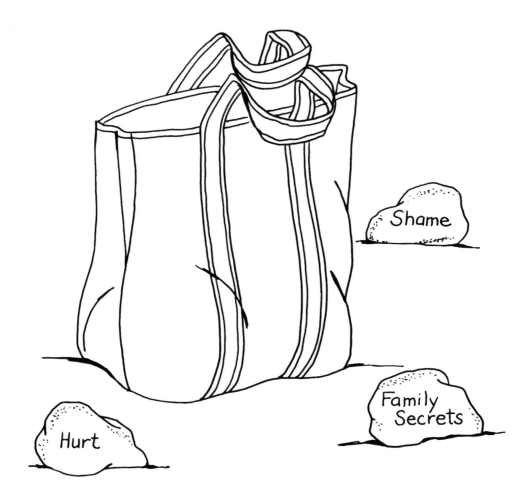

Example of Stuffed
Problems and Feelings

Feeling Puppet Family
(Ages 4 and up)

i

Children of all ages enjoy working with the puppets, especially six- to ten-year-olds. The puppets cast a magical spell on the children, enabling them to express anger, sadness, fear, and guilt.

DESCRIPTION

Angry Amy, Sad Sam, Fearful Frankie, Guilty Gail, Happy Harry and Confused Connie are the Feeling Puppet kids. They are sock puppets that children can easily manipulate. Each puppet has the initial of its respective feeling emblazoned on its tummy. The puppets live in a chemically dependent family. Mother and father puppets may be used interchangeably as the chemically dependent and co-dependent parents.

Using empty pop bottles to stand the puppets upright, they are placed in a semicircle. Each puppet has an identifying placard to help children remember its name. The group facilitators act out various problems between Mom and Dad puppets in two-to-three-minute sequences: confrontations about drinking and using drugs, verbal abuse, threats of divorce, and family fighting. Children then pick the puppets that best represent how they would feel if they lived in the Feeling Puppet Family. They share the puppet's feelings and tell why they feel that way. Children may take turns to be more than one puppet in the family.

EXAMPLE

Here are some comments from eight-year-olds who recently played this game:

Confused Connie, "Why does Daddy still drink when he promised me he would stop? I don't understand."

Happy Harry, "I'm happy when Dad drinks because then I get away with murder."

Guilty Gail, "If I just could be a better kid, I know my parents would stop using cocaine."

AFFIRMATIONS

"All of my feelings are okay."

"There are safe people I can talk to about my feelings."

COMMENTS

This is an extremely powerful activity to help children share feelings safely by communicating through puppets.

Ideally, each child takes a turn with each puppet to share a variety of feelings.

- Index card placards with the puppets' names
- Six empty pop bottles
- Eight sock puppets (see example below)

Example of feeling
puppets, Happy Harry
and Angry Amy

This activity is taken from *Kids' Power: Healing Games for Children of Alcoholics*

Guess My Feeling Game
(Ages 6 and up)

This fast-paced activity assists youngsters in identifying and expressing their feelings while at the same time developing congruency between their inner feelings and outer appearances.

DESCRIPTION

The facilitator begins the game by asking a volunteer to come forward and whisper a feeling in the facilitator's ear. The youngster then turns his or her back to the group. The facilitator directs the group to chant the magic chorus, "Turn, turn, turn in place, with a feeling on your face." As the group chants, the child slowly turns around and silently shows the feeling. After the expression is correctly identified, the child shares a time he or she experienced that particular feeling. The facilitator helps youngsters use "I" statements in sharing feelings.

This game works best when enough time is allotted to give each group member at least two chances to show a feeling to be guessed. The group facilitator follows up this exercise with a brief discussion about how we all have lots of similar feelings every day and that it's okay to talk about them with people we trust.

EXAMPLE

Lucy was extremely shy during the first day of family week, and had not spoken more than a handful of words. With some gentle prodding from the facilitator she finally did the Guess My Feeling Game with some help from the others. When the group correctly guessed "angry," Lucy whispered that she gets angry when Dad screams at her. Then she put her head down and quietly started to cry.

AFFIRMATIONS

"I can share my feelings if I feel safe."

"My feelings belong to me."

COMMENTS

An option here is to have youngsters look in a mirror after they put their feeling faces on. This is a powerful way for kids to develop congruency on the outside for the feelings they experience on the inside.

Assist shy youngsters in doing this exercise by offering to do it with them. After they've tried it once, they are usually ready to go solo the next time.

Sometimes it's necessary to give a child some assistance, not only in picking a feeling but also in creating the facial expression that can go along with it.

Stuck in the Feelings Game
(Ages 6 and up)

A kinesthetic exercise filled with fun and movement, Stuck in the Feelings demonstrates how people get weighed down by holding on to their feelings. This activity also provides specific strategies on how to lessen the load by identifying and expressing feelings in a regular way.

DESCRIPTION

Following a brief discussion about feelings (activities such as Feelings Alphabet or A Brainstorm of Feelings work well here), the facilitator asks for three volunteers to each role-play a different feeling. Initially the facilitator plays the star to demonstrate how the game works. With a self-stick note on each volunteer to represent the feeling each is playing, one by one the feelings approach the facilitator and identify themselves. Sometimes a feeling has to actually touch or gently shake the star to make its presence known, as people can be oblivious to their feelings at times. As each feeling introduces itself the star explains that it isn't safe to talk about feelings and stuffs that feeling inside by placing the child playing it behind himself or herself. Soon the star has all three feelings hidden. Instructing the feelings to lock arms and for the one closest to the star to grab hold of his or her arm, the star attempts to walk away but must carry all the stuffed feelings, as well. This is Stuck in the Feelings.

Now the facilitator asks a group member to be the star and three others to play the feelings. The game continues until everyone has had a chance to get weighed down and stuck by keeping many feelings inside. This activity powerfully demonstrates how people get bogged down by carrying so many repressed emotions.

EXAMPLE

Sevilla struggled mightily as "fear," "mad," and "sad" held on to her. She wiggled and moved about but couldn't get free. Finally this bright eleven-year-old yelled, "I don't want to do this anymore." Upon questioning from the facilitator, Sevilla shared, "I don't want to be heavy anymore. I just want to be a kid." The group offered comfort and support as she described sadness about how this activity reminded her of what happens at home.

AFFIRMATIONS

"I have choices, I can share or hold on to my feelings."

COMMENTS

Follow up with Share 'em or Stuff 'em, an exercise which gives group members specific tools about sharing feelings.

Ask each child playing a feeling to describe a time he or she felt that way. This helps the group get more practice in identifying and expressing feelings.

MATERIALS

• Post-it™ brand self-stick notes
• Markers

Feelings Mate
(Ages 6 and up)

A large group movement exercise that solidifies the new information and skills which youngsters have learned, Feelings Mate is a fun way to end the discussion on expressing one's feelings. It can be played many times over the course of a few minutes. Above all, it emphasizes the important concept that all feelings are okay.

DESCRIPTION

Each group member picks up an index card that has been placed face down on the floor by the facilitator. Each card has a feeling written on it, such as happy, sad, surprised, scared, excited, mad, or hurt. The facilitator instructs the children not to let anyone see their cards. Each feeling card has a corresponding card somewhere on the floor. The facilitator makes sure that each child can identify the feeling on his or her card and act it out nonverbally. The facilitator assists group members as needed.

With the children standing in a large circle the facilitator shouts, "Ready, set, go feelings!" The youngsters move about the room silently communicating their particular feelings with body language, facial expressions and other forms of nonverbal communication. Making their way around the room, the youngsters search for another person acting out the same feeling. After they discover their feeling companion, the children lock arms and walk together, still pantomiming the feeling. As they approach the facilitator, he or she must correctly guess the feeling they represent. When everyone has found their feelings mate, the game is complete. It may be repeated several times, then followed up with a brief discussion on feelings.

EXAMPLES

As the group members moved around the room they assumed various poses. Becky clutched her stomach as if she were in terrible pain. Carlos jumped about in delight. Billy sat in a corner with his lower lip curled and clenched fists covering his eyes. On the other side of the room, Macki had a stern look and shook a threatening finger at everyone who passed. Some held their body language and facial expressions while others burst out laughing. Soon everyone had found his or her mate. A rich discussion on feelings followed.

AFFIRMATIONS

"All my feelings are okay."

"I can share my feelings with safe people."

COMMENTS

Repeat this activity many times so youngsters can experience a wide range of feelings.

If an odd number of children are in group the facilitator will have to play.

Allow time for processing at the end of this activity. Give youngsters a chance to share those feelings that were the hardest and easiest to act out. Also discuss what feelings youngsters experienced while playing the game.

MATERIALS   • Index cards with feelings written on them.

Note: Make sure each feeling used is written on two index cards. The total number of feelings used must be half the number of group members playing.

Feelings Wheel
(Ages 6 and up)

With a spin of the wheel children find themselves in the land of feelings. An exercise designed to promote the expression of emotions, Feelings Wheel helps youngsters to communicate in new and exciting ways. Along the way comes the realization that feelings are okay and that sharing them with safe people is healthy.

DESCRIPTION
The children sit in a circle on the floor with the Feelings Wheel in the middle. The wheel is made of cardboard and has a metal fastener in the middle to make a spinner. The wheel is divided into eight spaces, each with a different feeling. Four of the feelings are comfortable ones (such as happy, glad, calm, excited, surprised, or joyful), and four are uncomfortable ones (such as sad, hurt, angry, ashamed, scared, or lonely).

One by one the children spin the wheel and then share a time they experienced the feeling on which the spinner stops. After a child shares a particular feeling, others may also tell about a time they felt that way. After two or three rounds the facilitator begins a discussion about how people experience lots of different feelings each day and how we often feel better when we share our feelings with others. This activity not only gives youngsters validation for their feelings but also helps them to realize they are not alone.

EXAMPLE
When the spinner landed directly on anger, Jimmy hesitated momentarily then blurted out, "I'm so angry at Mom for not wanting to be married to Dad anymore. I hate her." The facilitator asked this twelve-year-old if he wanted to do some work on this feeling. With the group's support, he was able to unravel a couple layers of his anger.

AFFIRMATIONS
"I can honestly express my feelings."

"Feelings are friends to identify and share with others."

COMMENTS
The facilitator should also participate in this activity to point out its value and importance for the group.

This has proven to be a good closing activity for feelings exploration.

MATERIALS

- A feelings wheel divided into eight feelings with a metal fastener in the middle to make a spinner. (See example on next page.)

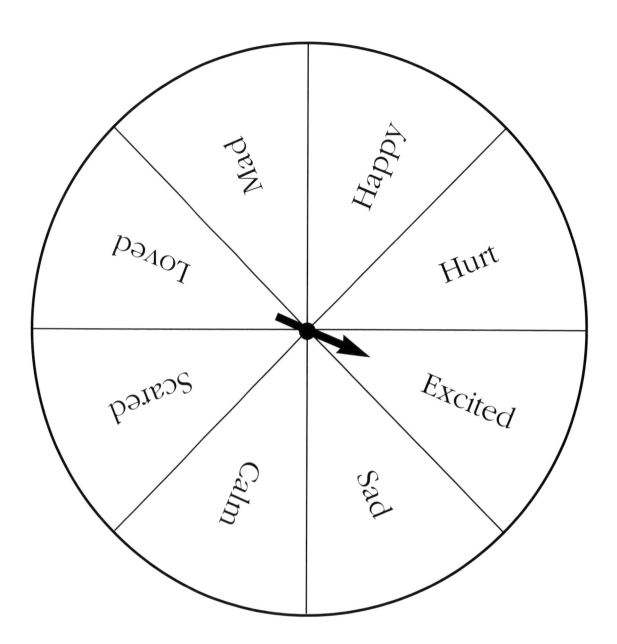

Example of Feelings Wheel

A Bag o' Feelings
(Ages 7 and up)

A Bag o' Feelings helps children to further develop the skills of expressing and taking responsibility for their feelings. It stresses that everyone has many different feelings everyday and that all feelings are okay.

DESCRIPTION
With the group sitting on the floor in a circle, the facilitator puts a brown paper bag in the middle. Prior to group the facilitator has filled the bag with an assortment of index cards, each with a feeling and a face depicting that particular feeling. The leader explains that every day people have lots of different feelings and that the key is learning how to deal with them.

The facilitator shakes the bag, picks an index card, identifies the feeling, and shares a time he or she felt that way. Other group members can then describe a time when they had that same feeling. After the first turn is complete, the next person shakes the bag, pulls a card, and shares an occasion when he or she experienced that feeling. The game continues around the circle and everyone has the opportunity to participate. A discussion follows about the importance of sharing feelings with people you trust.

EXAMPLE
Aaron, a shy nine-year-old who didn't participate much in group, reluctantly put his hand in the bag o' feelings to pull out a card. He looked at the card and muttered, "Sad," as he then let out a long sigh. With some encouragement from the facilitator, Aaron whispered, "When my Dad moved away I felt sad." Tears rolled down his cheeks and he nodded affirmatively when asked if he still missed his Dad. Aaron had taken a big step, and he received much support and validation.

AFFIRMATIONS
"I can learn new things about feelings."

"Today I will share my feelings with someone I trust."

COMMENTS
If time allows, do two or three revolutions around the group. This gives the participants the opportunity to share a variety of feelings firsthand.

Draw a feeling face on each card next to the feeling so that youngsters who have trouble reading can still benefit from this experience.

Remember to stress that all feelings are okay and that talking about them with safe people is an important way for children to take care of themselves.

MATERIALS
- Brown paper bag
- Index cards, each with a feeling and a corresponding feeling face

Artwork
(Ages 4 and up)

Many children enjoy drawing pictures with markers and crayons. Often kids have difficulty talking and sharing feelings about their family problems. Some experience guilt and anxiety over what can seem like betraying their parents and the family secrets. Art is a powerful yet less threatening way for youngsters to begin sharing on a feelings level. Children can also have fun in the process.

DESCRIPTION

With colored pencils, markers, and crayons spread across the floor, the facilitator asks the children to draw a picture illustrating family problems. If necessary, the facilitator may give more specific instructions such as, "Draw a picture of something you are scared or angry about in your family." Group members are instructed that they don't have to share their drawings with anyone if they so choose. As the children work on their pictures, the facilitator roams around the room and allows each youngster to explain his or her picture. (The facilitator should not attempt to analyze any of the drawings.) Even the scribbles of a preschooler have a definite story behind them if the facilitator takes the time to ask.

When the children have finished, the facilitator gives each one an option to share his or her creation with the group. A discussion ensues as group members describe the problems and feelings they see in the pictures shared. The facilitator not only validates the youngsters' feelings but also emphasizes that all feelings are okay. Children also come to see that they have experienced many similar problems and that they are not alone.

EXAMPLE

Stefano worked vigorously on his picture in the far corner of the room. Usually quiet and reserved, this six-year-old was the first volunteer to share his picture with the group. A huge face that took up the whole page had big, sad eyes in the middle that were crying. A caption crammed on the side said it all: "Don't do drugs, Dad." Everyone was touched by Stefano's sadness and pain.

AFFIRMATIONS

"It's okay to share my feelings with people I trust."

"My feelings belong to me. It's my choice to hold them or share them."

COMMENTS

Let children know that their pictures will not leave the group room. This assurance gives them the safety to really work from their hearts.

Artwork is a powerful window into children's lives. Take the time to talk with each child individually about his or her creation.

For many of these kids a picture is truly worth more than a million words, because they can draw what they can't say. (See sample drawings on next page.)

MATERIALS

- Paper
- Crayons, markers, and colored pencils

Examples of
children's artwork

The Feelings Place
(Ages 6 and up)

This activity gets children up and moving as they explore the vast environs of the land of feelings. On their journey youngsters have the opportunity to identify and express a variety of emotions. They also learn that they can experience more than one feeling at a time.

DESCRIPTION   Strategically situated around the group room are feeling regions, Lonely Land, Sad State, Angry Area, Happy Haven, Fear Forest, Shame Station, and Hurt Hideout. Each region is clearly marked with a poster stating its name, with a corresponding feeling face above it (see illustration). The safari begins as the facilitator and the children roam the wilderness in search of feelings. As each feeling region is discovered the group stops and each person shares a time he or she felt that emotion. As the journey continues through each region, the facilitator acknowledges and validates every person's feelings and stresses that all feelings are okay and normal.

After all lands have been discovered, the group sits on the floor in the middle of the room. The facilitator puts a deck of index cards face down in the middle of the circle. The cards each feature a scenario for the youngsters to think about, such as being picked on by a school bully, parents fighting, having a big birthday party, or a parent drinking alcohol. The facilitator selects a child to choose an index card and read it to the group. After a few seconds the facilitator asks the children to go to the feeling region that represents how they would feel if this situation really happened to them. The youngsters scurry about the room until they find the appropriate region for themselves. The facilitator visits each land to ask the youngsters why they stopped there. The game continues until each child has had a chance to read a scenario from the index cards.

EXAMPLE   No matter what scenario the index card described, Becka faithfully headed to Happy Haven. The other children were spread among the various feeling regions, and often Becka was alone. At the end of the activity Becka shared that she always, always felt happy inside. The facilitator asked, "What about when Mom rages at you?". The smile quickly disappeared from Becka's face and her eyes filled with tears. With the support of her peers she walked ever so slowly to Fear Forest. The facilitator explained that it's okay to feel afraid sometimes; it's okay to feel lots of different feelings.

AFFIRMATIONS   "Feelings are my friends. I can listen to them."

"I can have more than one feeling at a time."

COMMENTS   After each scenario is read the children may need enough time to visit more than one feeling region. The facilitator can explain that it's okay to have more than one feeling at a time.

The facilitator may need to assist younger children in reading the scenario on the index card.

MATERIALS
- Posters with feeling designations and matching feeling faces
- Index cards with various scenarios

Example of Feeling Regions Posters

SAD STATE

HAPPY HAVEN

FEAR FOREST

Feelings Face Case
(Ages 7 and up)

Designed to introduce youngsters to a wide variety of feelings, this work sheet reinforces the concept that all feelings are okay. The feeling faces serve as a reminder that humans can have many different emotions on a daily basis. Children largely share from their own experiences as they write captions for each of the faces.

DESCRIPTION

After a brief discussion on feelings and an activity such as the Feelings Wheel, the facilitator passes out the Feelings Face Case work sheet to each group member. Instructed to write a caption for each facial expression, youngsters discern the feeling each face represents and then write an appropriate caption based upon it. The facilitator moves about the group and checks in with each youngster, offering any assistance the children may need to complete this activity.

After everyone has finished writing, youngsters have the option of sharing a caption they wrote for any particular facial expression. A discussion follows in which group members relate an occasion when they have had a similar expression, describing the circumstances and the feelings that accompanied that expression. The activity is concluded by talking about the freedom that comes from letting go of feelings by sharing them with safe people.

EXAMPLE

Carlos, Joann, and Earl were amazed to discover that they each wrote a similar caption for the angry face. In their own words each had written, "I hate the divorce." After talking about their anger all three were relieved to know that others had experienced the same situation and feelings in their lives. "I guess I'm not the only one," Joann said with a sigh. Earl and Carlos nodded in acknowledgment, and a thin smile crossed Earl's face.

AFFIRMATIONS

"Everyone experiences lots of feelings each day."

"Feelings are road signs that guide me on my way. I can pay attention to them."

COMMENTS

Youngsters can work on this exercise in pairs. This option can help facilitate the socialization process for kids.

The facilitator should remind youngsters that it's okay to ask for help with this exercise and that he or she is available for that purpose.

MATERIALS

• Feelings Face Case work sheets (see example on next page)
• Pencils with erasers

FEELINGS FACE CASE

What feelings do you suppose each person is experiencing? Why do you suppose they are having those feelings?

Feeling: _____

_____

_____

_____

Feeling: _____

_____

_____

_____

Feeling: _____

_____

_____

_____

Feeling: _____

_____

_____

_____

Feeling: _____

_____

_____

_____

Feeling: _____

_____

_____

_____

Feeling: _____

_____

_____

_____

Feeling: _____

_____

_____

_____

Feeling: _____

_____

_____

_____

Feeling: _____

_____

_____

_____

Our Common Bond, Feelings
(Ages 6 and up)

This exercise helps youngsters to see that they are not alone when it comes to the difficulty of expressing uncomfortable feelings. It also teaches them how they can support one another in so doing and become safe people with whom others can talk. Above all, this visual and kinesthetic activity is lots of fun.

DESCRIPTION

With the children sitting on the floor in a circle, the facilitator asks them to think about a feeling or two they had been holding inside before they entered the children's program. The facilitator passes a ball of yarn to a group member and asks that child to share one of those feelings. After doing so, the child wraps the loose end of the yarn around one finger and then rolls the ball of yarn across the circle to another group member. This person continues the process by sharing a stuffed feeling, wrapping the loose end of the yarn around one finger, and then rolling the ball across the circle to another group member. Before long, everyone in the group will be connected by the yarn, a tangible representation of their similar experience, holding uncomfortable feelings inside.

The weaving and intersecting lines of yarn represent how confused and jumbled up people feel inside as a result of stuffing feelings. The facilitator instructs one child to tug a little on the line, and things get tight and uncomfortable for everyone, just like one stuffed feeling can create the pressure and tightness that leads to stomachaches. The facilitator points out that by helping and supporting one another, talking about uncomfortable feelings becomes easier.

EXAMPLE

Rafael was particularly moved by this exercise; it was the first time he had ever heard other kids talk about being angry at their parents. "I thought I was bad for getting angry at my parents. I thought I would go to hell," this eleven-year-old shared. "Now I get that it's okay to get mad as long as I don't hurt myself or others." Rafael smiled as the group leader nodded affirmatively.

AFFIRMATIONS

"All feelings are okay, even uncomfortable ones."

"Safe people can help me in sharing my feelings."

"My feelings belong to me. It is my choice to share them or hold them."

COMMENTS

Follow up this game with Feelings Wheel, as children are now usually prepared to share from a deeper feelings level.

The group leader may actively participate in this game by sharing an uncomfortable feeling he or she has difficulty expressing. This is good modeling behavior.

MATERIALS

• Ball of yarn

Share 'em or Stuff 'em Game
(Ages 4 and up)

This kinesthetic activity helps children to understand that their feelings belong to themselves. Moreover, it empowers youngsters with the choice of sharing or holding their feelings inside. Time is spent on identifying safe people with whom to talk to about their feelings.

DESCRIPTION   The group facilitator asks for a volunteer to demonstrate the game. The youngster tells the group about a feeling, such as anger, hurt, fear, sadness, or happiness, that he or she commonly stuffs inside. With a bit of magic the facilitator becomes that very feeling and gently takes hold of the child, either around the ankle, arm, or shoulder. The volunteer is instructed to walk around the room but must drag the stuffed feeling wherever he or she goes. The child experiences the pressure and stress of carrying around pent-up emotions. The facilitator momentarily stops the game and asks the group what they have observed. A discussion follows about how the volunteer isn't free to play and have fun when he or she carries feelings around, about how tired the person becomes, and how the child can never completely forget the feeling, even though he or she tries very hard to do so.

The game resumes with the volunteer again lugging the stuffed feeling around the room. The youngsters clearly come to see that the feeling belongs only to that person. The facilitator explains that the child can either hold this feeling or share it. With that, other group members begin to shout, "You look like you need to talk. C'mon let's talk." When the volunteer finally states, "Hey, I need help. Right now I feel scared," to another group member, the stuffed feeling lets go of the child and its intensity diminishes. A brief discussion follows on how sharing feelings with people you care for and trust helps to free you to take good care of yourself.

The facilitator asks for another volunteer and the game proceeds until everyone has had a turn. Each youngster faces the challenge of sharing or stuffing feelings. The choice is clearly theirs.

EXAMPLE   Erin attempted to move about the room with "sadness" draped over her. After five minutes of huffing, and puffing, and barely moving Erin decided to hold on to her feeling. The facilitator nodded and asked her how she felt. She replied, "I am very tired. I just want to lie down now." The facilitator looked directly into her green eyes and gently asked, "Isn't that how you feel most of the time, Erin?" Although she didn't immediately respond, the message clearly got through to her.

AFFIRMATIONS   "My feelings belong to me."

"It's my choice to share or hold my feelings."

Never make a value judgment if a youngster chooses to hold his or her feelings. Instead, point out situations when it is healthy to hold feelings, such as when there are no safe people around, or when a person needs time to sort out his or her feelings.

CHAPTER 8

Wednesday

Taking Care of Me — Problem Solving and Self-Care

KEY CONCEPTS
- Taking good care of myself is my most important job.
- It's okay to ask for help.
- There are safe people and places to help me.
- My body belongs to me - it's okay to say "no" if someone touches me in a way I don't like.
- It's okay to tell a safe person about someone touching me in a way I don't like.

GOALS
- To explore a variety of ways to take good care of oneself and stay safe.
- To develop insight about appropriate people and places to turn to for help.
- To learn and practice a variety of problem solving and coping strategies.
- To understand the differences between appropriate and inappropriate touch and to develop healthy physical boundaries.

ACTIVITIES
Jeopardy, The Self-Care Game

Self-Care Bags

Self-Care Wheel

Safe/Unsafe People Game

Safe People Maps

STARR Problem Solving Model

Problem and Solution Game

Boundary Junction

Safe Way Role-Play

Alphabet Soup Revisited

Sailing the Seven *C*s

Problem Sheets

Searchin' Serenity

Taking Care of Me Game

Space Invaders

BOOKS/STORIES   *No-No the Seal*

An Elephant in the Living Room

The Secret of the Peaceful Warrior

I Can't Wait

The Mouse, the Monster, and Me

I Would Prefer Not To

FILMS   *Twee, Fiddle, and Huff*

Lots of Kids Like Us

SONGS   "Logical" by Peter Alsop (*Take Me With You* cassette)

"My Little Clock" by Peter Alsop (*In the Hospital* cassette)

"My Body" by Peter Alsop (*Wha' D' Ya Wanna Do* cassette)

"If I Was In Charge" by Peter Alsop (*Pluggin' Away* cassette)

"All It Takes Is a Friend" by Jim Newton (*Friends of the Family* cassette)

"It's Alright To Ask For Help" by Jim Newton (*Children At Heart* cassette)

"One Day At a Time" by Jim Newton (*Children At Heart* cassette)

DAILY THEME

Mini-Lecture

Children from addicted and/or codependent families often grow up too fast, a result of assuming adult problems, worries, and concerns. They may be overwhelmed and confused by all that is happening around them and to them. While most of these children manage to survive, they get caught in a family trap where no one consistently models healthy living skills. Rather, some family members usually try to take care of one another instead of themselves, which causes a paucity of self-care modeling. Children attempt to deal with complex life problems with only a few items in their "toolboxes" and with few healthy examples to follow. The absence of a consistent role model adds to their sense of confusion and they often feel alone. Many experience feelings of guilt and shame as a result of failing to solve the family's problems. While these youngsters survive, they can pay a large price in the process.

To help children learn to cope with and overcome these problems, facilitators can take the following steps:

1. Introduce children to a variety of problem solving and coping strategies. Help them to realize that everyone has problems to face and solve each day. Youngsters dealing with addiction and/or codependency issues may have several difficult problems to handle. Moreover, children may also experience difficulties in relationships with friends, neighbors, and at school. By learning new self-care and problem solving tools, children are more able to cope positively with their lives. The children's group can be a safety net where youngsters can test and practice different ways of successfully handling problems. They come to see that the most important job for kids is to take care of themselves.

2. Assist youngsters in understanding that it's okay to ask for help, and that doing so is a sign of strength, not weakness. Explain that there are many safe people in their communities who will provide support and assistance if asked to do so. Give children maps detailing what makes certain people safe and others not; children of addiction are notorious for picking the wrong people with whom to share. Introduce the notion that youngsters don't have to handle their problems alone, and that others can help them take better care of themselves. Just by talking with others, kids can come up with good ideas and solutions.

3. Guide children in realizing that they have options in handling life problems and taking good care of themselves. Such a process helps youngsters develop choices for ways to positively cope, adds new items to their toolboxes, and increases their self-confidence. Emphasize that a major key in self-care and problem solving is to always stay safe, an essential way for children to take care of themselves. An option here is to introduce kids to the concept of boundaries, especially physical boundaries. Help them to see that their bodies belong to them and that it's not okay for others to touch them in any way the children don't like.

By introducing youngsters to basic problem solving and self-care strategies, facilitators empower youngsters to focus on themselves and to take good care of themselves in the process.

Jeopardy, the Self-Care Game
(Ages 8 and up)

Combining the fun and excitement of a familiar television game show with learning basic self-care concepts, Jeopardy teaches youngsters a variety of ways to take good care of themselves. This game is played in a context of teamwork and cooperation where everyone wins.

DESCRIPTION

The facilitator divides the group into two teams and asks each one to select a group name. Once completed, the facilitator introduces the five Jeopardy categories by writing them on newsprint or on a greaseboard in the front of the room. The categories for the self-care game are body, mind, feelings, spirit, and being a kid. The facilitator explains that these are the areas for kids to focus on when taking good care of themselves. Giving each team paper, pencils, and a clipboard to write on, the facilitator instructs them to brainstorm self-care ideas in each area. The facilitator moves between the groups and offers support, suggestions, and encouragement. Ten minutes usually suffices for this part of the activity.

Now both groups sit in front of the newsprint or greaseboard and the facilitator serves as the host. After everyone hums the Jeopardy theme song, the game begins. Starting with the body category, each team takes turns suggesting a self-care strategy for that topic. The facilitator writes each appropriate response under that category heading. The facilitator may also offer suggestions to assist the children in this process. The game continues until it weaves its way through the mind, feelings, spirit, and being a kid topics. The object of the game is to fill the newsprint or greaseboard with ideas for taking good care of oneself. A discussion follows in which the facilitator describes how youngsters may be in jeopardy if they fail to take the necessary time for self-care.

EXAMPLE

Aubrey, usually very quiet during group, didn't seem very excited about playing Jeopardy. She started to get interested during the laughter and giggling as everyone hummed the theme song. With encouragement she participated in her team's discussion. Somehow she felt safer participating in the smaller group. With each suggestion she made, Aubrey's confidence grew. Aubrey contributed a variety of self-care ideas. "This is fun," she shared during the discussion. "I really do have lots of good ways to take care of myself." She beamed as a smile filled her face.

AFFIRMATIONS

"It's important for me to take good care of myself."

"I deserve to take good care of myself."

"It's okay to ask for help. I don't have to do things all by myself."

COMMENTS

Follow up this game with Self-Care Bags. Having self-care ideas on the newsprint or greaseboard lends itself to this activity.

Stress the importance of learning from one another in this game. The purpose of creating teams is to make the groups smaller and emotionally safer, yet the object is for the teams to collectively fill the board with good ideas.

MATERIALS
- Newsprint or greaseboard
- Markers
- Paper
- Pencils
- Clipboards

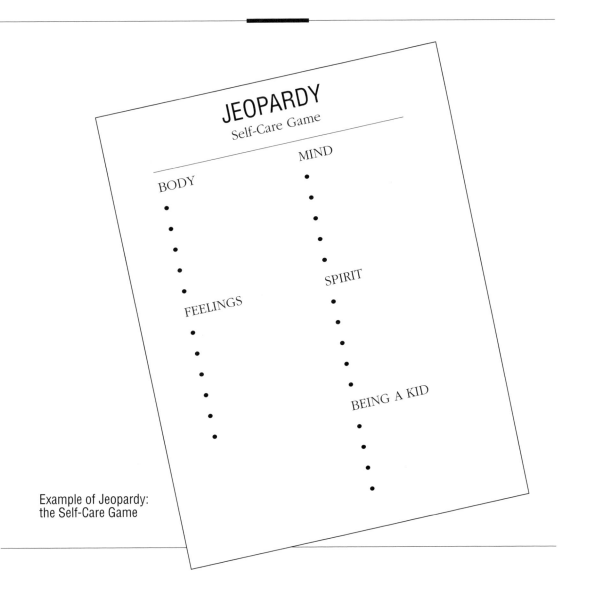

Example of Jeopardy:
the Self-Care Game

Self-Care Bags
(Ages 7 and up)

This exercise empowers children to incorporate self-care strategies into their daily lives. One of the few activities youngsters actually take home with them, self-care bags remind kids of the importance to take time out for themselves because they are worthy and deserve it.

DESCRIPTION   The facilitator distributes small lunch bags and instructs the children to decorate them. They may do so with crayons, colored pencils, and markers in any way they like, just as long as each child writes his or her name on the bag. Have plenty of extra bags available in case someone makes a mistake or ends up not liking his or her design. Youngsters usually need twenty minutes or so to complete the activity, but the facilitator should give the group extra time, if necessary, to create bags they are proud of.

After the bags are finished, the facilitator hands each youngster seven index cards. Using the results from the Jeopardy Self-Care Game on the newsprint or greaseboard (see Jeopardy Self-Care Game in this section), the facilitator asks the children to write down a self-care idea on each side of the seven index cards. Youngsters have visual cues in the areas of body, mind, feelings, spirit, and being a kid from the Jeopardy game to use as ideas to write on the index cards. The facilitator tells the group to write suggestions for each of the areas listed above so that youngsters will be sure to include ideas for taking good care of their bodies, minds, feelings, spirits, and the little kid inside each of them.

After the children have completed this phase, the facilitator instructs them to put their completed index cards into their care bags. Sitting in a circle, the children, one by one, take out a card and read each side for self-care ideas. The facilitator explains the importance of having a suggestion on each side, as children have choices in how they can take care of themselves.

A discussion ensues about the importance of caring for oneself. The facilitator brainstorms with the group ways that they can use their bags when they get home: If you're ever bored or not feeling very good about yourself, pull a card out of the bag and follow the instructions; use your self-care bag on a daily basis.

EXAMPLE   Suzie looked very sad after getting into an argument with another group member during break. As she acknowledged her sadness to the facilitator, she took his suggestion of pulling a card out of her self-care bag. She didn't like the suggestion on one side, "Play a game." On the other side it said, "Tell someone your feelings." After a few moments of contemplation Suzie told the group, "I feel sad when people call me names." A rich discussion followed as this ten-year-old really did take care of herself.

"I can take good care of myself."

"I deserve to take good care of myself."

"I can make good choices to take care of me."

This activity works very well as a follow-up to Jeopardy, the Self-Care Game.

Use the self-care bags throughout the rest of the week to help the group practice using them to take care of themselves.

MATERIALS

- Small lunch bags
- Crayons, markers, colored pencils
- Index cards

Self-Care Wheel
(Ages 6 and up)

A take-off on a popular television game show, this activity helps children to further develop self-care skills. While it stresses teamwork and cooperative learning, youngsters particularly enjoy the fun and excitement the Self-Care Wheel generates. Throughout this exercise the message "it's important to take good care of yourself" comes across loud and clear.

DESCRIPTION

Divide the children into two teams and ask each to select a team name. After the teams are introduced, a volunteer from each one spins the wheel and lands on a particular letter of the alphabet, A-J (see illustration). Each team then looks at the self-care game board to identify the specific self-care skill to discuss, such as exercise, play, or share feelings (the game board contains two self-care strategies from each of five important areas, body, mind, feelings, spirit, and being a kid). The team discusses ways they use this skill in their own lives and brainstorms new applications as well.

The facilitator emphasizes the importance of practicing self-care on a daily basis as he or she moves between the two brainstorming teams and offers suggestions and feedback. When everyone is ready, the first team presents its findings to the group. The other team offers additional ideas and personal experiences. After the first team is finished, the second team makes its presentation. The game concludes with a brief wrap-up discussion.

EXAMPLE

The Purple Power team landed on the share feelings self-care strategy. Luke, Wendy, Earl, and Juanita came up with an impressive list of ways to build this skill into their daily lives, including a variety of safe people with whom to talk. When asked how they presently share feelings, the team quickly fell silent and their eyes shifted to the floor. After a long silence, Wendy spoke up. "I really don't share my feelings much. I hold them in," confided this honest ten-year-old. "I feel sad about that." The facilitator pointed out that she had just shared her feelings with the group. A smile appeared on her face and she replied, "Yes, I guess I really did."

AFFIRMATIONS

"I am learning new ways to take care of myself."

"I am a wonderful and beautiful kid."

"It's okay to take good care of myself."

COMMENTS

Repeat the game a few times to allow each team to consider a variety of self-care skills.

Avoid competition by stressing teamwork and cooperation. Youngsters can learn the valuable lesson that others can provide additional help and guidance.

This activity works well in conjunction with the Safe People Maps presented later in this chapter.

MATERIALS
- Spinning wheel
- Self-Care Game board

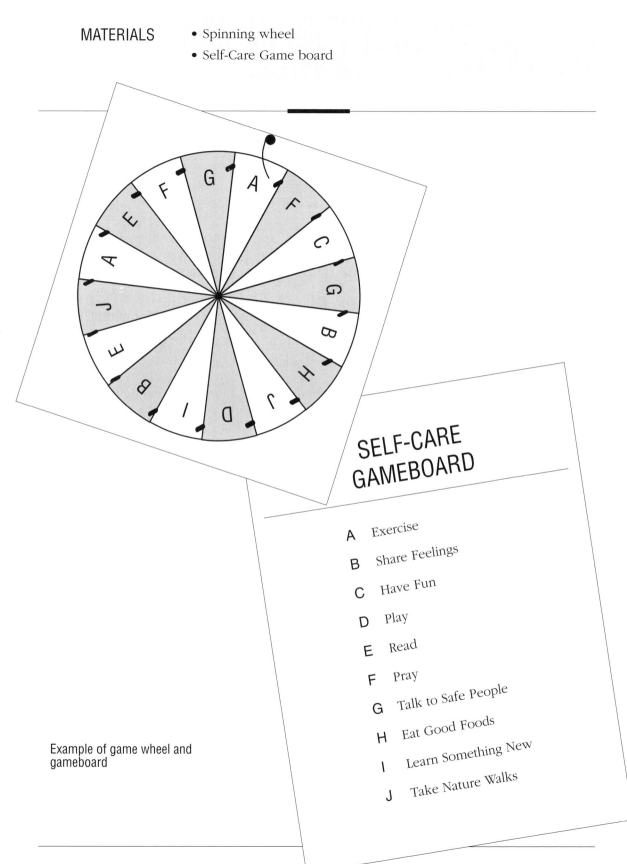

SELF-CARE GAMEBOARD

A   Exercise

B   Share Feelings

C   Have Fun

D   Play

E   Read

F   Pray

G   Talk to Safe People

H   Eat Good Foods

I   Learn Something New

J   Take Nature Walks

Example of game wheel and gameboard

Safe/Unsafe People Game
(Ages 6 and up)

In this activity youngsters learn specific information on what makes certain people safe and others unsafe. By giving children maps of safe people, facilitators empower kids to seek out people who can really provide support, guidance, and assistance. This important life skill can serve youngsters for many years to come.

DESCRIPTION

With the group sitting in a circle in the middle of the room, the facilitator initiates a brief discussion about safe people, describing characteristics that make someone safe and others that don't. The facilitator writes the words *Safe People* on newsprint or a greaseboard and asks the group to brainstorm exactly what behaviors make someone safe.

To deepen this process the facilitator explains that he or she will be role-playing a variety of people over the next several minutes. The facilitator will walk outside the room and come back in playing someone else, either a safe person, an unsafe person, or someone in-between. After a few minutes in character the facilitator will say, "Stop," and the children guess if that person was safe, unsafe, or somewhere in-between. A brief discussion follows as the group attempts to list other characteristics of safe people. The facilitator plays five or six different characters, running the whole spectrum from safe to really unsafe (exhibited by such behaviors as yelling, being disrespectful, touching inappropriately by grabbing a child's shirt, and not really listening to them). If time allows a group member may volunteer to role-play another character and then the group decides if that person was safe or unsafe. The facilitator completes this activity by reviewing the Safe People list and seeing if the group can make any final additions to it.

AFFIRMATIONS

"It's okay to ask safe people to help me."

"I can learn about what makes someone safe."

"I will pick safe people to help me."

COMMENTS

Follow up this activity with Safe People Maps, an excellent game that can logically be integrated here.

During the role-plays use a variety of characters, some clearly safe and unsafe, as well as others in-between. This will facilitate a rich group discussion.

MATERIALS

- Newsprint or greaseboard
- Markers

Safe People Maps
(Ages 7 and up)

This activity assists youngsters in deepening their awareness and understanding of what makes certain people safe and others not so safe. By consciously searching for characteristics of safe people, children soon have maps to determine whom they can turn to in times of need.

DESCRIPTION

During one of the initial group sessions, the facilitator introduces the concept of safe people. Children discuss whom they turn to when they need support and guidance. More important, they begin to ponder what it is that makes that person safe. Taking a large piece of newsprint with *Safe People* written on the top and taping it to the wall during each session, the facilitator guides a brief discussion about characteristics that help make someone safe. At first, even six-year-olds share two things about safe people: they don't laugh at you when you ask for help, and they don't blab what you tell them to just about everyone.

By taking five minutes near the end of each group, children can add new data based on the concepts and learning that have taken place during that session. Before long this exercise becomes spontaneous as kids yell out new characteristics as soon as they come to mind. For example, Robbie contributed the idea that safe people aren't always drinking or using other drugs. Lucy added that safe people often share their feelings with others, including her.

Toward the end of the weeklong program, the list contains numerous characteristics. The facilitator takes ample time during one of the last groups to have the children brainstorm who in their lives has many of these gifts and skills (probably no one has them all, because no one's perfect). This exercise helps youngsters to identify the safe people in their lives. The facilitator provides extra support for those who have trouble translating the list into people in their lives. Finally, everyone gets a copy of the list (Safe People Map) and is encouraged to add to it as they go through life.

EXAMPLE

At the end of a group devoted to feelings, Barry quickly raised his hand when it came time to discuss new characteristics for safe people. This twelve-year-old floored the group facilitators with this astute observation: "Safe people listen with their eyes. They really show they care." Barry greatly added to the richness of the list and certainly gave the facilitators something to think about.

AFFIRMATIONS

"I can learn about safe people."

"There are safe people I can turn to for help."

COMMENTS

If this process bogs down at all, do it in conjunction with the Safe/Unsafe People Game; this latter activity spurs several thoughts and ideas about safe people and their many characteristics.

The facilitator may guide the process by helping youngsters touch upon any important points that escape them about safe people.

MATERIALS
- A sheet of newsprint with *Safe People* written at the top
- Masking tape
- Markers
- Safe People Maps

Example of a
Safe People
Map

SAFE PEOPLE MAP

Safe People
- Listen to me
- Don't laugh at me
- I can trust them
- Don't always drink and use Drugs
- Really care about me

SAFE PEOPLE

SAFE PEOPLE MAP

Starr Problem Solving Model
(Ages 7 and up)

Youngsters are introduced to a basic and simple problem solving model to take good care of themselves. This approach works well because each child is a STARR, truly a one-of-a-kind, precious individual capable of learning new ways to handle life's problems.

DESCRIPTION

The facilitator begins by asking the group to describe problems they have recently experienced. Asking for a volunteer to describe how he or she solved a particular problem, the facilitator guides the group in a discussion on the process of solving problems and introduces children to the STARR method.

The facilitator hands out copies of the STARR Problem Solving Model (see example at the end of this game). The facilitator names and describes the five basic steps while writing them on a greaseboard or newsprint in the front of the room. The facilitator encourages group discussion throughout the steps, especially the next to the last one, resources to help. The group leader emphasizes that it's not only wise to get help from others in solving problems but also very smart to find a safe place to hang out when a problem becomes too dangerous or difficult to handle.

The group goes back to the problems they shared at the beginning of this activity and attempts to solve them utilizing STARR. Such practice helps youngsters feel more comfortable with this particular model and increases their confidence in successfully applying it.

EXAMPLE

Earl applied the STARR method to his problem of getting picked on at school. As the group collectively worked on this dilemma, Earl realized what had been missing in his previous attempts. "I tried to do it by myself and it didn't work," confided this shy eleven-year-old. The group brainstormed a variety of people who could help, yard duty person, counselor, teacher, principal, or the grandma with whom Earl lives. Although still a bit uncertain, Earl was learning that asking safe people for help is okay, a concept that previously had been foreign to him.

AFFIRMATIONS

"It's okay to ask for help."

"I can make good choices to solve problems."

COMMENTS

Facilitators may reintroduce the STARR model throughout the remainder of the week so that children can resolve any problems or difficulties that arise in group.

MATERIALS

- Copies of STARR Problem Solving Model
- Newsprint or greaseboard
- Markers--

STARR PROBLEM SOLVING MODEL

STOP   What is the problem?

Name it.

THINK   How do I feel?
How can I solve this problem?

Identify options.

ACT   Choose the best option that helps me stay safe and allows
me to take good care of myself.

RESOURCES   Who can help me?
Where can I find assistance?

Find safe people and places for help.

REVIEW   Would I try to solve this problem the same way again?
What would I do differently next time?

Problem and Solution Game
(Ages 6 and up)

This activity helps youngsters integrate basic problem solving skills into their everyday lives. The Problem and Solution Game provides an atmosphere of teamwork and cooperation conducive to building such skills. Children also have fun in the process of practicing these important life tools.

DESCRIPTION

Using the STARR Problem Solving Model as the preceding exercise, the facilitator presents three or four problem scenarios on index cards. Dividing the group into two teams and having each pick a card, the facilitator walks the youngsters through STARR to solve their problems, such as fighting with siblings or being embarrassed by a parent's behavior. The facilitator guides each team in brainstorming possible options and their consequences by listing them on a greaseboard or newsprint in front of the room. Youngsters are encouraged to explore a wide array of choices that allow for safety and resolution. The facilitator also lists the group's suggestions of resources to help, those safe people and places to turn to for support and guidance.

A discussion follows about the best two or three solutions to the problem. Here the facilitator again emphasizes the concept of choice, as there are many choices to make in solving problems. The key is enabling youngsters to master the STARR method and thereby build their self-confidence.

EXAMPLE

As a result of this exercise Timmy learned that pouring out Dad's alcohol wasn't a good choice in staying safe when his father got drunk. Even though his method never worked, Timmy had stubbornly repeated it. During the Problem and Solution Game he got many different options for solving his problem, such as playing with a friend, telling someone he trusts about his feelings, staying in his room and listening to music, or going somewhere he feels safe. Timmy now had some alternative ways to take care of himself. He smiled at this prospect, even if it didn't mean that his dad would stop drinking.

AFFIRMATIONS

"I can learn new ways to solve problems and take better care of myself."

"There are safe people and places to help me."

"I have choices about solving problems and staying safe."

COMMENTS

Ask younger kids to draw the different options and possible consequences in resolving their dilemmas. This will facilitate the process of choosing the best solutions.

Allow the children to do the work in the brainstorming phase. Provide comments and feedback only when necessary. The most important function is to guide the youngsters through the process.

- Three or four index cards with problem scenarios
- Newsprint or greaseboard
- Markers
- Copies of STARR Problem Solving Model

Example of STARR Problem sheet

STARR PROBLEM SOVING MODEL

STOP

What is the problem?

Name it. *Kids call me names at school*

THINK

How do I feel? *Sad and hurt*
How can I solve this problem? *Walk away*
tell them to stop
call them names
Identify options. *get a teacher*

ACT

Choose the best option that helps me stay safe and allows me to take good care of myself. *Walk away*
if it does not work tell the teacher
teacher or bes friend

RESOURCES

Who can help me?
Where can I find assistance?

Find safe people and places for help.

REVIEW

Would I try to solve this problem the same way again? *Yes*
What would I do differently next time?

Mabeye get the teacher first

119]

Boundary Junction
(Ages 6 and up)

An activity that introduces children to the concept of boundaries, Boundary Junction teaches youngsters about their own physical space. It also provides a variety of suggestions about what to do when others violate this space.

DESCRIPTION   With the children sitting in a large circle around the perimeter of the room, the facilitator asks for a volunteer to demonstrate this exercise. Standing in the center of the circle, the child is instructed to shout "Stop!" when the facilitator gets so close to him or her that the youngster feels uncomfortable. The facilitator walks directly toward the volunteer and halts when the child yells. The facilitator checks with the youngster to ascertain if this is a safe distance, because sometimes the child asks the facilitator to take a step backward or forward. Then the facilitator puts masking tape on the floor at the point where he or she finally stopped. This exercise is repeated from both sides and the back, with the facilitator always halting at the child's request. Masking tape is put on the floor at each vantage point, forming a box that clearly represents that youngster's personal space. The facilitator directs the child to walk around his or her space to get comfortable with it belonging only to him or her. Then, the facilitator attempts to enter the volunteer's space, and the group offers suggestions to the child about taking care of himself or herself, such as walking away, telling the person to stop, or telling someone else about it.

Repeat this activity until everyone has had a chance to experience and see his or her personal space. Each time the group offers safe suggestions about what to do when the facilitator crosses a youngster's physical boundaries. A designated group member writes the comments on a greaseboard or newsprint for everyone's viewing. Finally a discussion follows about how boundaries keep us safe and how maintaining this physical space is a great way to take care of ourselves.

EXAMPLE   At first Joey didn't know what to do when the group leader walked into his space. This seven-year-old just stood there with a perplexed and frightened look on his face. With the group's support he finally bellowed a loud "No!" each time the facilitator violated his physical boundaries. The group applauded enthusiastically when he stood up for himself.

AFFIRMATIONS   "I can learn to take good care of myself."

"My body belongs to me. It's not okay for people to touch me in ways I don't like."

"There are safe people and places to help me take good care of myself."

COMMENTS   The facilitator may repeat this exercise by role-playing a stranger, a raging parent, or a best friend. This helps children to see that their physical boundaries can vary from person to person and circumstance to circumstance.

Follow up this activity with a discussion on appropriate vs. inappropriate touch.

An excellent story to present in conjunction with this activity is "No-No the Seal."

MATERIALS

- Masking tape
- Greaseboard or newsprint
- Markers

Safe Way Role-Play
(Ages 6 and up)

Used in conjunction with many of the other activities in this theme, Safe Way Role-Play lets youngsters demonstrate their burgeoning problem solving and self-care skills. Many children especially enjoy practicing these skills in the context of skits.

DESCRIPTION

This game is an excellent follow up to such activities as the Self-Care Wheel, the Problem and Solution Game, or Boundary Junction, where youngsters are actively involved in problem solving and staying safe. The facilitator divides the group into two teams and asks each one to demonstrate a safe solution to a problem they just discussed. The facilitator makes sure each team works on a different problem scenario and stresses that there are different safe choices in resolving each dilemma.

The teams form huddles at opposite ends of the room to prepare their role-play solutions. The facilitator, offering support, suggestions, and enthusiasm, roams back and forth between the two groups, giving the youngsters twenty minutes or more to come up with their skits. Once ready, each team presents its skit to the other group. A discussion follows on how each team arrived at its particular solution, as well as on other safe solutions that could work. Emphasis is placed on safe people and places that could assist in problem resolution.

EXAMPLE

The New Kids team role-played the situation of a child being stuck in the middle between her parents. As the drama unfolded, the parents were fighting when their child came into the room. "Which one of us is right?" the mother asked the little girl. With slight hesitation the girl responded, "I don't know. I'm just a kid and I love you both." The New Kids came up with an excellent solution. Not only did they enjoy doing the role-play but they also learned from one another in the process.

AFFIRMATIONS

"I can learn new ways to solve problems and take good care of myself."

"It's okay to ask for help."

"I deserve to treat myself well."

COMMENTS

This change-of-pace activity gets kids actively involved in the learning process.

Role-plays enable youngsters to demonstrate the many new skills they've learned, as well as to practice them.

This is a good exercise to end the day's theme on problem solving and self-care strategies.

MATERIALS

• Assorted props for the role-plays (a bag of clothes, wigs, and assorted items will suffice)

Alphabet Soup Revisited
(Ages 7 and up)

This activity goes beyond helping youngsters understand that family addiction and codependency are not their fault. While this game helps children know in their hearts that they are not responsible for their parents' problems, it also guides them in learning how they can take good care of themselves. Youngsters come to realize that self-care is ultimately their most important responsibility.

DESCRIPTION

The facilitator distributes the updated Alphabet Soup Revisited sheets (see example at the end of this activity) to group members. One by one youngsters volunteer to read one of the Seven *C*'s. The children briefly discuss the meaning of each *C* and share how it applies to their lives before moving on to the next *C*. The facilitator then explains that the Seven *C*'s can actually be divided into two parts, things you are not responsible for (the first three *C*'s) and things you are (the final four *C*'s). A discussion follows in which the group differentiates between these two categories. The facilitator reiterates that children can't make their parents' problems better but that they can learn to take care of themselves.

Now youngsters can either color their Alphabet Soup Revisited sheet with crayons and markers or draw a picture on the back of the sheet. The pictures can either illustrate how family addiction really isn't the children's fault or show a new way children can take good care of themselves. Another option, if time permits, is to divide the Seven *C*'s among group members and have them make collages illustrating the message of each *C*. Youngsters paste the pictures and words they cut out of magazines onto large poster boards. During group discussion, children look at the various collages and guess which *C* each one represents.

EXAMPLE

Frankie had difficulty playing Alphabet Soup Revisited. He told the group facilitator that he was very angry he had to do a collage about *CELEBRATE* me. "It's not fair. Why can't I do one on can't *CONTROL* or can't *CURE?*" this twelve-year-old bluntly asked the facilitator. Not getting the response he wanted, Frankie sat in a corner and stared off into space. After a few minutes had passed, the facilitator approached Frankie and validated his anger. "It's real hard for you to let go of Mom's problems and just focus on yourself," the facilitator gently offered. Tears quickly welled up in Frankie's eyes as he nodded affirmatively. Even though he never completed the collage, he clearly got the point of this exercise.

AFFIRMATIONS

"It's important to take good care of myself."

"I can let go of my parents' problems."

"I'm learning about what I'm responsible for and what I'm not."

Whether children draw pictures or make collages, hang the artwork on the walls during subsequent sessions. It will serve as a powerful visual reminder of exactly what youngsters can and can't do in their daily lives.

It's often necessary, particularly with younger children, for the facilitator to provide extra assistance and support as the group members work on their drawings and/or collages. Simply roaming around the room and checking in with each child can make a big difference.

MATERIALS

- Alphabet Soup Revisited sheets
- Crayons and markers
- Poster board
- Magazines
- Scissors
- Glue

(The last four items are for the collage option.)

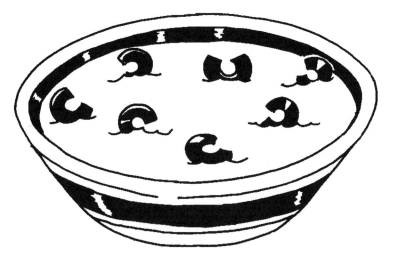

ALPHABET SOUP REVISITED

It's important for kids from addicted families to remember the 7 C's

The 7 C's:

- I didn't CAUSE it.
- I can't CONTROL it.
- I can't CURE it.
- But I can learn to take CARE of myself

by—
- COMMUNICATING feelings.
- Making healthy CHOICES and
- CELEBRATING myself.

Sailing the Seven C's
(Ages 7 and up)

An excellent follow up activity to Alphabet Soup Revisited, Sailing The Seven C's helps youngsters further deepen their understanding that they're not responsible for their parents' problems. This role-play exercise also solidifies specific skills children can use to take good care of themselves. Kids, up and moving as they tap into their creativity, have some fun along the way.

DESCRIPTION   The facilitator writes the Seven C's from Alphabet Soup Revisited on newsprint or a greaseboard. As a review, children read one *C* at a time and the group discusses what each means and how it applies to their lives. After this process the facilitator draws a line between the third and fourth *C* (see illustration) to differentiate between what youngsters can't (take care of the parents' problems) and can (take care of themselves) do. Once this is clearly established, the game is ready to begin.

The facilitator demonstrates how this activity works. He or she leaves the room for a moment and re-enters role-playing a scene illustrating one of the seven *C's*. After a one-minute skit, the group guesses which *C* was being portrayed. After performing a few role-plays for the group to see how it is done, the facilitator asks for volunteers to do role-plays depicting the various *C's*. While some youngsters go solo, others work in small groups. Learning by doing helps to deepen group member's grasp of this important information. After each scenario, a brief discussion takes place to make sure everyone understands what has just transpired.

EXAMPLE   Bonnie and Jenna teamed up to do a scenario. As they came into the group room, Jenna confided, "Well, Mom and Dad are out drinking again. Let's clean the house so maybe they'll stay home tomorrow night. We can even dump out all the liquor." Bonnie thought about this for a few moments and then shook her head no. "Right now I'm scared and angry they're not home. Let's call Uncle Frank to help us." She picked up the phone and pretended to call her uncle. "He's coming over right now," Bonnie told Jenna excitedly. The girls had actually demonstrated two different *C's*, communicating feelings and making healthy choices by calling Uncle Frank for help.

AFFIRMATIONS   "I can learn new ways to take care of myself."

"Today I'll let my parents take care of their own problems."

"There are safe people and places to help me."

COMMENTS   The initial scenarios that the facilitators perform should be simple and obvious. This allows youngsters to build confidence in their abilities, giving them more motivation to volunteer to do their own role-plays.

If necessary, the facilitator can help group members plan possible role-play situations.

Allow adequate time to discuss each scenario to make sure everyone is on the right track.

MATERIALS
- Greaseboard or newsprint
- Markers

Example of Sailing the Seven C's poster

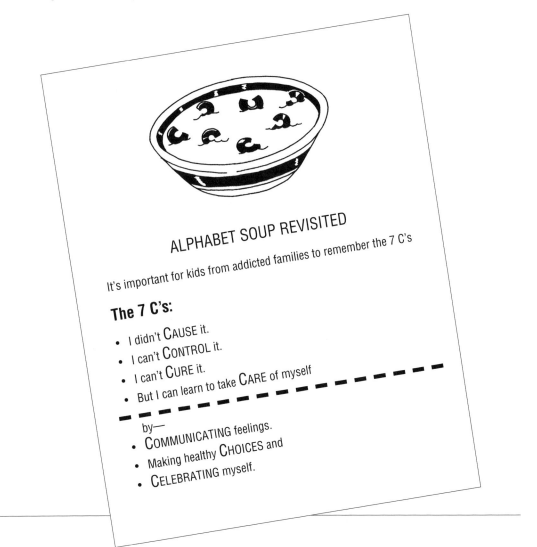

ALPHABET SOUP REVISITED

It's important for kids from addicted families to remember the 7 C's

The 7 C's:
- I didn't CAUSE it.
- I can't CONTROL it.
- I can't CURE it.
- But I can learn to take CARE of myself

by—
- COMMUNICATING feelings.
- Making healthy CHOICES and
- CELEBRATING myself.

Problem Sheets
(Ages 7 and up)

This activity may be incorporated as a supplemental exercise to most others in this theme. It features a variety of common problems youngsters face in their daily lives. The group may practice their newly developed skills in resolving these dilemmas and taking good care of themselves simultaneously.

DESCRIPTION

The facilitator may elect either to divide the group into teams or have everyone work collectively on this exercise. Passing out a problem sheet to all group members, the facilitator asks youngsters to read each problem scenario. The children quickly see that the dilemmas are those they are already familiar with, such as getting bullied, parental fighting, the threat of separation and divorce, broken promises, and not being listened to are but a few examples. The facilitator assigns each team or the group to tackle certain problem situations.

The facilitator gives the group or teams five-to-ten minutes to discuss the particular dilemma they are focusing on and brainstorm possible safe solutions. With a youngster designated to record the various safe choices to resolve the problem, a discussion ensues and the many options are recorded on newsprint or a greaseboard for all to see. The group discusses the relative merits of each solution, and the facilitator pipes in with suggestions and feedback as appropriate. Special attention is focused on safe people to whom youngsters could turn for assistance.

EXAMPLE

The group struggled with the problem scenario of parental separation, because many of the children were presently dealing with this situation. For more than ten minutes they worked feverishly trying to make things better for their parents. Finally the facilitator chimed in, "Kids don't make parents separate or make them get back together. It's not the kids' job." Silence fell over the room as more than one youngster's eyes welled up with tears. The group was now ready to tackle this problem on a feelings level.

AFFIRMATIONS

"I have choices in taking good care of myself and solving problems."

"I don't have to do it alone. I can ask others for help."

"It's okay to put myself first in solving problems."

COMMENTS

If youngsters get stuck with any particular problem, have them use the STARR Problem Solving Model to get back on track.

Offer children lots of praise and encouragement in their efforts. The more they become comfortable with the process the easier it is for them to integrate it into their daily lives.

- Problem Sheets
- Greaseboard or newsprint
- Markers

PROBLEM SHEET

Picked on by bully

Parents fighting

Broken promises

Possible separation or divorce

No one listening to you

Nothing to do, bored

Put downs by siblings

Asked if you want alcohol or cigarettes

Difficulty getting homework done

Searchin' Serenity
(Ages 7 and up)

This activity helps youngsters to see the Serenity Prayer in an entirely new light. It provides clarity in assisting children to understand the importance of taking good care of themselves. The prayer also can serve as a valuable frame of reference in handling tough problems while staying safe.

DESCRIPTION

The facilitator, after a brief discussion on problem solving strategies, hands out Searchin' Serenity work sheets to all group members. It's often quite helpful for children to work in small groups so they may learn from one another. The facilitator proceeds by reading the first part of the prayer and asking the teams to quietly brainstorm what things in their lives they can't change. After five minutes or so a large group discussion ensues and the facilitator writes the various teams' responses on newsprint or a greaseboard for all to see and comment on.

Next the facilitator reads the middle section of the prayer and asks the teams to brainstorm those things in their lives they can change. After a few minutes the large group assembles and the facilitator records the various responses on the newsprint or greaseboard. If the group doesn't do so, the facilitator emphasizes that the most important things kids can change are themselves.

With this in mind the facilitator reads the last part of the prayer and asks each team to come up with plans to take good care of themselves. Again the group comes together and the responses are recorded for all to see. The facilitator stresses that a wise person is someone who truly takes good care of himself or herself. A discussion follows.

EXAMPLE

While the group was trying to differentiate between what they could and couldn't change, Ben put it all into perspective. This bright ten-year-old commented, "When it rains outside, that's something I can't change. But I can put on a raincoat and umbrella to deal with it. That's what I can change." The group was momentarily silent and then heads nodded approvingly. Ben had captured the essence of this exercise.

AFFIRMATIONS

"I can take good care of myself."

"I am worthy of treating myself well."

"Others can help me stay safe."

COMMENTS

Use the Searchin' Serenity exercise to help youngsters resolve dilemmas through the rest of the week. It will help children focus on themselves.

This activity works well in conjunction with Problem and Solution game, Problem Sheets, or Safe Way Role-Play.

MATERIALS

- Searchin' Serenity sheets
- Newsprint or greaseboard
- Markers

When my parents get into fights I play with my dog to have fun so I play and stay safe.

SEARCHIN' SERENITY

God, grant me the serenity to accept the things I cannot change

Here are some things I can't change (others):

1. _____
2. _____
3. _____
4. _____
5. _____

Courage to change the things I can

Here are some things I can change (me):

1. _____
2. _____
3. _____
4. _____
5. _____

And the wisdom to know the difference

Here is a plan to take good care of me:

1. _____
2. _____
3. _____
4. _____
5. _____

Taking Care of Me Game
(Ages 7 and up)

Youngsters are faced here with some difficult problems. Working in a cooperative fashion, they brainstorm a variety of ways to resolve the dilemmas and especially how to take good care of themselves in the process.

DESCRIPTION

The facilitator randomly divides the group into two teams, the Actors and the Solvers. Before the session the facilitator has written different problem scenarios, each on a separate index card. Now he or she pulls a card from a bag and hands it to the Actors. They have five minutes to prepare a spontaneous portrayal of the specific problem. Problems include doing poorly at school, feeling lonely, parental fighting, and being offered alcohol or other drugs.

The Actors bring the problem to life, and then the Solvers have five minutes to brainstorm different options to successfully solve the problem and stay safe. The facilitator lists their solutions on newsprint or a greaseboard for all to see and ponder. A group discussion follows about other possible choices to resolve the dilemma in a healthy manner. Once a problem has been adequately discussed, the Actors and the Solvers switch places and another problem is tackled.

EXAMPLE

The problem situation was parents getting drunk. The Actors brilliantly portrayed this scene, in which the little boy was quite scared with all the yelling and fighting. Moved by this graphic visual, the Solvers suggested that the kid pour out all the booze when no one was around. After much discussion the children realized that this wasn't a good solution because the little boy could get hurt for throwing out the alcohol. Joey, eight years old, blurted out, "You mean I can solve problems and take care of myself at the same time!" Such a revelation put this activity on a whole new level.

AFFIRMATIONS

"I can make good choices in solving problems."

"It's okay to think of myself first."

"It's important to always stay safe."

COMMENTS

This activity works well because it gets youngsters actively involved in learning by doing.

Play this game a few times so everyone has a couple of turns as an Actor and a Solver.

MATERIALS

- Index cards with problems written on them
- Paper bag
- Newsprint or greaseboard
- Markers
- Bags of props (optional)

Space Invaders
(Ages 7 and up)

An advanced version of Boundary Junction, this visual activity helps youngsters to claim their personal space. It also helps them to realize that their individual boundaries can change depending upon the person involved, that person's mood, their own mood, and the particular circumstances. Most important, Space Invaders empowers children with specific skills and strategies to use when others invade their boundaries.

DESCRIPTION

Using the experiences gained from Boundary Junction, the facilitator reviews the concept of personal space. Taking this concept a step further, the facilitator asks for a volunteer to demonstrate the various levels of space that individuals require. With the volunteer standing in the center of the room, the facilitator will role-play six different people in succession, each time approaching the volunteer until he or she calls out, "Stop!" as an indication that the person is getting too close. Upon hearing "Stop!" the facilitator puts a small strip of masking tape on the floor and writes the role-played person's name on the tape for easy reference. For example, the facilitator may role-play a drunk mother and write those words on the tape at the spot where the volunteer yells "Stop!"

The depth of this experience is dependent on the facilitator's knowledge of each child's family history and dynamics. Among the six role-plays could be a loving mom, raging dad, drunk parent, caring dad, acting out sibling, abusive parent, best friend, safe adult, and unsafe adult. The facilitator's ability to plug in the most relevant scenarios depends on really knowing each youngster well. Children are amazed to see the scope and extent of their boundaries depending on the circumstances. This is particularly true with the difference between a loving parent and that same parent screaming and yelling. Once the six boundaries are set, the facilitator picks one and quickly turns into a space invader by trespassing the volunteer's personal boundary. The volunteer offers three different strategies for coping with space invading, such as yelling, running away, screaming "No," getting help, calling a safe person, yelling "Stop," or telling someone you trust about what just transpired. Once complete, a brief discussion takes place about the volunteer's boundaries and strategies for handling the space invader. Repeat the process until each youngster has had a chance to volunteer.

EXAMPLE

Lennie was amazed to see how close his mom can get when she's kind and loving, yet how far he wants her away when she's drunk and raging. "Move about ten more steps back when you're like that," he told the person role-playing his mom. As his voice rose and his eyes widened, Lennie yelled, "Get away. Don't hurt me. I hate it when you drink and throw things. Stop." Lennie fought back tears as the facilitator froze in his tracks. Lennie was really learning about the importance of protecting himself when his mother drank too much.

"I am learning to take good care of myself."

"It's important for me to stay safe."

"Having boundaries helps me to protect myself."

Refrain from making value judgments about youngsters' boundaries. Facilitators can learn much about group members from this exercise.

Briefly process information between each child's turn. Valuable feedback and discussion often takes place, especially in terms of developing strategies to cope with Space Invaders.

- Masking tape
- Markers

Thursday

I Am Special — Self-Worth

KEY CONCEPTS
- Everyone has special qualities, even family members with addiction or codependency problems.
- I am one of a kind. There's no one in the world exactly like me.
- It's okay to feel good about myself.

GOALS
- To increase awareness that every person is one of a kind with special qualities.
- To explore and discover individual's special qualities and gifts.
- To celebrate the unique beauty and worth of each child.

ACTIVITIES
Living Cards

I Am Special Bags

Dressing For Dinner

A V.I.P., That's Me

My Great Plate

Affirmation Sensation

My Special Collage

Letter Special

The Car Wash

Inside Special

BOOKS/STORIES
What's So Special About Me? I'm One of a Kind

Liking Myself

That's What Friends Are For

FILMS
Lots of Kids Like Us

Twee, Fiddle, and Huff

DAILY THEME

Mini-Lecture

Children growing up with addiction and/or codependency often have very little to celebrate. Many problems, so typical in these family systems, such as drinking, drugging, family fights, and a lack of attention pose incredible barriers. Physical and sexual abuse, as well as verbal violence, can also damage youngsters' burgeoning sense of themselves. Many of these children feel guilty, embarrassed, and ashamed. The belief that "my family is different and I must keep it a secret" leads many youngsters to believe that something is seriously wrong with themselves as well. Such a powerful message can result in low self-esteem and self-worth in children, making them vulnerable for the seeds of addiction and codependency to be sown. While the family and home play crucial roles in a youngster's developing self-esteem, the family's attention in such situations is inconsistently directed to the children, which only adds to the belief that "there really is something wrong with me." Consequently, self-esteem and self-worth fail to fully blossom and youngsters, learning all too well from the family system, tend to look outside themselves for answers.

The focus here is to assist children in enhancing their sense of worth and promoting positive feelings about themselves. As children develop healthy self-images they can begin a new legacy of health and wellness. Emphasize that everyone has special qualities, even practicing addicts and codependents, their disease just hides them much of the time. Stress to all group members that they are rare and precious, truly one of a kind people . Inform the kids that they are going on a treasure hunt today to discover the special beauty and goodness they have inside. Help them to understand that they are special simply because they are, not just because of what they do or don't do. Help them to see that it's okay just to be themselves and to celebrate so doing. Celebrating doesn't involve bragging, judging, or putting others down but instead using the many gifts with which they have been blessed. Keep in mind that initially it will be easier for many youngsters to see the special qualities in others than in themselves. With some time and practice it will become easier for children to own and celebrate their gifts.

Living Cards
(Ages 8 and up)

This powerful exercise in peer affirmation is incredibly helpful in promoting self-esteem. If at all possible, do this exercise on the floor. Kids get more out of Living Cards if they sprawl across the room. Play some of their favorite music softly in the background.

DESCRIPTION

Have the children find places on the floor with plenty of room. Give each of them a piece of white paper (8½" x 11"). Spread crayons, colored markers and pencils across the floor. Ask each child to write his or her name in the middle of the page. Encourage the children to be creative with different colors and specialized lettering (e.g., block or script). Then ask them to reflect silently on the special qualities everyone contributes to the group. No one does any writing yet. (Because the kids have been with one another in group this shouldn't be difficult.) The facilitators can provide a few examples to help people get started.

After a few minutes, the children pass their papers to the left, and their neighbors write briefly about the special qualities of the person whose name is on the sheet. This continues until each paper has gone around the group and come back to the owner. Take time for each group member to absorb the special things that have been written about him or her. Then everyone has a chance to share his or her Living Card with the others. Ask how each child feels about the comments on his or her card. Children may take their Living Cards home. Many hang them in their rooms; others have them framed (see sample card at the end of this activity).

EXAMPLE

Ten-year-old Steven was having a rough time. He believed he couldn't do anything right and didn't fit in. He wanted to go home. During the Living Cards exercise, others wrote about his courage, swimming ability, and friendliness. When Steven read his card, he lit up like a Christmas tree. He came to see himself in a new way. His eyes filled with tears when he told the group, "Thanks, I guess I really am okay."

AFFIRMATIONS

"Everyone has special qualities."

"I am a beautiful and special person."

"It's okay to feel good about myself."

COMMENTS

This activity works with younger kids if the facilitators write for them. A variation on this theme is to have the little ones draw a picture of what's special about the others, such as a flower, the sunshine, a rainbow, or a favorite toy.

Despite concern that group members might write derogatory comments about one another, we have rarely seen this happen. The facilitators must set the tone for this exercise by sharing, and they must also participate with their own cards.

MATERIALS
- White paper
- Crayons
- Colored pencils or markers
- Tablets of paper

Example of
Living Card

This activity is taken from Kids' Power: Healing Games for Children of Alcoholics

I Am Special Bags
(Ages 6 and up)

This simple activity helps youngsters to discover the buried treasure they possess inside. Children especially enjoy reflecting to group members their specialness while basking in the warm reflections sent by the others.

DESCRIPTION

The facilitator passes out lunch bags and decorating materials to the group and instructs the children to decorate their bags and put their first names on them. The facilitator allows fifteen minutes or more for this activity. Have extra bags available in case youngsters make a mistake or don't like their final creations. After the children are finished, the facilitator collects the bags and lines them up at the front of the room. Each child is then given several blank index cards, and the facilitator instructs the group to write a special quality of each group member on a separate card and then to drop it into that person's bag.

Once everyone's bag is full, the facilitator gives the group a few minutes to read their cards. The facilitator asks each child to share a compliment or two from his or her bag. A discussion follows about how everyone has special qualities and that it's okay to feel good about oneself. Then the children write the words "I am special" on their bags. They may take their bags with them as a reminder of all their special qualities.

EXAMPLE

Rosa, a quiet and shy seven-year-old, methodically checked the contents of her bag. Surprisingly she wanted to share two of her gifts with the group. Rosa uttered very softly, "Smart and kind." A thin smile appeared on her face as the others clapped and cheered for her. It was the first time she had ever really smiled in group.

AFFIRMATIONS

"I can celebrate my special qualities."

"It's okay to feel good about myself."

COMMENTS

Have younger children draw something special about each person in group. Employ this strategy as well for youngsters who have difficulty with reading and writing activities.

Make sure that each member does a card for every other person in group. Help youngsters to realize the importance of this activity by making sure the facilitators decorate a bag and fully participate as well.

MATERIALS

- Lunch bags
- Decorating materials (markers, crayons, construction paper, scissors, and glue)
- Blank index cards

Dressing for Dinner
(Ages 6 and up)

A fun, high-energy exercise, Dressing for Dinner helps youngsters to own and celebrate their many special gifts. It also provides practice in the skill of giving and receiving compliments.

DESCRIPTION The group forms a large circle on the floor. The facilitator puts a chair in the center and asks for a volunteer to discover his or her many special qualities. Once that person is seated, the facilitator passes out adhesive-backed computer labels and markers to the other group members. Their task will be to think of something special about the volunteer and write it on a label. (Note: It is often helpful to brainstorm a large list of special qualities on newsprint or a greaseboard as a prelude to Dressing For Dinner.) After everyone has written down one of the volunteer's qualities, the facilitator shouts, "Go!" and the group proceeds to stick the labels all over the volunteer. Prior to this activity the facilitator has set guidelines that no labels may be placed on a person's face or near his or her private parts. This activity continues until everyone, including the facilitator, has been covered with special qualities.

The room is filled with joy, giggles, and laughter during the first half of this activity, but the real test comes now. The facilitator instructs the children to roam around the room; every time they get close to another group member and make eye contact they must read to that person two of the special qualities he or she is wearing. In return that person tells the other child about two of his or her gifts, and the person responds with "Thank-you". The facilitator concludes the exercise after approximately five minutes of roaming.

EXAMPLE Becky learned very quickly how much easier it was to give compliments than to receive them. "I feel embarrassed when others say that stuff about me," she told the group. Much to her amazement she saw others nodding as she spoke. During the ensuing discussion Becky learned that she was not alone. Somehow this understanding made it easier for her and the others, too.

AFFIRMATIONS "Everyone has special qualities."

"I can give and receive compliments."

"It's okay to celebrate my special qualities."

COMMENTS At the conclusion of the exercise give each child a piece of blank paper on which to put his or her labels to keep as a memento of this special event. The sticky labels come off quite easily.

Sometimes it helps to give youngsters a snack to enjoy as they roam around the room. Choose healthy snacks like fruit or carrot sticks.

MATERIALS

- Labels
- Markers
- Newsprint or greaseboard
- Paper
- Snack (optional)

A V.I.P., That's Me
(Ages 6 and up)

Combining the fun and excitement of a television talk show with an exploration of the special and unique gifts children possess, this activity assists youngsters in celebrating their beauty and goodness. This exercise also helps children to accept compliments from others and to own all of their qualities.

DESCRIPTION

The group room is set up like a talk show, complete with a red carpet (a red velour bath towel works fine) and a special V.I.P. chair with a big star on it. The facilitator, who serves as the program host, chooses a youngster to be the show's producer. The producer practices holding up "CLAP" and "CHEER" placards for the studio audience. This adds to the fun and excitement. The audience sits on the floor a few feet from the talk show set and will clap and cheer at the producer's beckoning and also on their own accord.

The facilitator explains that the host only interviews very important people. He or she briefly describes how everyone in this group possesses many wonderful and different qualities; the purpose of the V.I.P., That's Me program is to celebrate these special gifts and people. Asking for a volunteer to be today's first guest, the facilitator welcomes this child to the show and asks for name, age, and city where he or she lives to get things rolling. The facilitator then focuses on the youngster's special gifts: kindness, creativity, humor, athleticism, honesty, intelligence, listening skills, etc. The host chooses two of these and asks a question about each one, such as, "Have you always been a fast runner?" or "Where did you learn to be such a good listener?" Three members of the studio audience can then add another quality they've noticed about the V.I.P.. A final cheer for the V.I.P. concludes the show. Repeat this activity several times until all group members have had an opportunity to be the guest star.

EXAMPLE

Jaime acted like she really didn't want to participate in this activity. She sat in the star's chair with her arms folded and a very skeptical look on her face. This ten-year-old had been difficult to reach throughout the entire group experience. The studio host didn't make much of a dent but the audience sure did as the kids yelled, "fun," "smart," "pretty," "great at sports," and other nice compliments. Even though the comments exceeded the limit of three, the facilitator allowed things to continue as Jaime looked at the group in amazement. With just a little more feedback from the group, Jaime was sitting proudly and beaming a huge smile. "Can I have another turn right now?" she coyly asked.

AFFIRMATIONS

"I have many special gifts."

"I can celebrate me today."

Before starting this activity the facilitator can decide which special gifts he or she will point out to each child. This helps to avoid duplication and spur-of-the-moment thinking.

If time allows, the facilitator may also take a turn in the V.I.P. chair. Everyone in the studio audience can share one thing about the facilitator's special gifts.

Allow approximately five minutes per child to ensure adequate time for all concerned.

MATERIALS

- Red carpet or towel
- Two placards, one with "CLAP" and one with "CHEER" written on them
- A folding chair with a star taped on it
- Microphone (optional)

My Great Plate
(Ages 8 and up)

A spin-off on Living Cards, this lively activity gets youngsters up and moving as they communicate special qualities to one another.

DESCRIPTION

The facilitator spreads crayons, colored pencils, and markers across the floor, then hands a white piece of cardboard to each group member. As in Living Cards, the facilitator instructs the kids to creatively write their first name on the middle of the cardboard. It is helpful to provide a few finished products as examples (script letters, bubble letters, different colors) to spark group members' creativity. After the youngsters have completed their masterpieces the facilitator punches two holes at the top of each piece of cardboard, then gives the children yarn to put through the holes and instructs them to tie a knot so that the Great Plate can be worn around their necks. The facilitator provides assistance to children who need help tying their knots.

Wearing the plates around their necks the kids brainstorm a variety of special qualities, which the facilitator records on newsprint or greaseboard for all to see. This list provides the group with visual cues to assist them in completing the task in a meaningful way. After putting their placards on their backs and out of view, the children walk around the room with a marker and write a special quality on each person's plate. Often a long train develops as Jimmy writes on Lisa's plate and Shelly writes on Jimmy's plate and Manuel writes on Shelly's plate. Once completed, the train needs to shift positions and continue with other plates. The shifting often produces lots of giggling and laughter. Joy fills the air as kids simultaneously have fun and receive gifts.

Once everyone has written on each plate the group sits in a circle on the floor. With two minutes of quiet time to find the "buried treasure," the children turn their plates around and read about their own special qualities. Everyone has a chance to share a few items from their plates, and a brief discussion follows on accepting compliments.

EXAMPLE

Michael's Great Plate had really captivated him. As he scanned the many gifts others attributed to him, his eyes got wider and his smile broader. "I really get to take this home?" the eight-year-old asked. He giggled spontaneously when the group members nodded their heads.

AFFIRMATIONS

"It's okay to feel good about myself."

"I can celebrate my special qualities."

"I am a special and talented kid."

COMMENTS

This activity can work with younger children if they draw pictures to represent one another's qualities.

It's important for the facilitator to participate in this activity with the children.

MATERIALS
- White cardboard
- Hole punch
- Yarn
- Markers, crayons, colored pencils
- Newsprint or greaseboard

Affirmation Sensation
(Ages 6 and up)

This exercise introduces children to the healing power of affirmations. Youngsters are reminded of how capable, unique, and irreplaceable they truly are, giving them all the more reason to celebrate and take especially good care of themselves.

DESCRIPTION

The facilitator introduces the group to affirmations by displaying a variety of them colorfully written on index cards. A discussion follows about the role of affirmations in reminding youngsters to take good care of themselves and celebrate their special qualities and gifts. With the facilitator's assistance the group collectively brainstorms several affirmations, all of which are recorded on newsprint or greaseboard.

Finally, the facilitator passes out two index cards to everyone in group and asks the children to write a couple of affirmations for them to take home. Using crayons or markers, the youngsters may create a new affirmation, take one from the group's brainstorm list, or use one the facilitator had displayed to kick off the activity. The youngsters have plenty of time to choose their affirmations, write them down, and creatively decorate their index cards. A brief discussion ensues about how the children can use affirmations daily when they return home.

EXAMPLE

Lennie worked intently on his affirmation cards, putting much thought and effort into his creations. He proudly shared with the group, "I am enough, Hooray!" and "I can be free, it is up to me." Throughout the rest of the day Lennie occasionally dug into his pocket, pulled out the cards, and gazed at them. He understood how important they could be for him.

AFFIRMATIONS

"I am lovable and capable."

"I can create something wonderful for me."

"I deserve to take good care of myself."

"I can celebrate me."

COMMENTS

The youngsters can carry their new affirmations in their Self-Care Bags (see Wednesday's activities), if they so choose.

Refer to this exercise two or three times during the day by having the children read their affirmations when they need an extra boost of support or encouragement.

MATERIALS

- Index cards
- Markers or crayons
- Greaseboard or newsprint

My Special Collage
(Ages 6 and up)

This exercise helps youngsters to more fully appreciate that everyone has special qualities. It also deepens the children's abilities to own and celebrate their intrinsic beauty and worth.

DESCRIPTION

This activity serves as a powerful follow up to Living Cards, I Am Special Bags, or Dressing For Dinner, all exercises designed to get youngsters in touch with their many special qualities. After putting magazines, scissors, and glue within easy reach, the facilitator places a large poster board in the center of the group and explains how each member will contribute to My Special Collage. The children are first instructed to explore the magazines and to cut out pictures and words that depict their special qualities. After youngsters have had plenty of time to cut out representations for themselves, the facilitator asks the children to scan the magazines one more time, now searching for other members' special qualities. This enables each child to have a richer and fuller array of words and pictures. The facilitator should actively participate in this phase of the exercise.

Now the group begins putting their cut-outs on the large poster board. The facilitator describes how each member's words and pictures form a cluster, and how the clusters complement one another in filling out the board. The children negotiate with one another about where they'll put their individual clusters on the board. Quite surprisingly conflict rarely emerges, and the facilitator reiterates that everyone has special qualities. After the collage is finished the facilitator hangs it on the wall and everyone has a chance to describe his or her part of it. Amidst clapping and cheering for one another, the facilitator emphasizes the celebration at hand, as each youngster has special gifts, which make the poster board all the richer and fuller.

EXAMPLE

Lindsay looked sad when she only found three pictures that vaguely resembled her specialness. This eight-year-old didn't want to finish the activity. With a little prodding, Lindsay somewhat reluctantly asked the group for help. As a chorus of "That's easy," and "No problem" filled the air, the children produced eight cut-outs in no time, much to Lindsay's surprise. She started to sit up taller and participated more actively for the rest of the day.

AFFIRMATIONS

"Everyone has special qualities, especially me."

"It's okay to feel good about myself."

"I can celebrate me."

COMMENTS

Be sure to have a wide array of magazines depicting the racial and ethnic backgrounds of all group members.

The facilitator must carefully observe this process, supplementing the pile of cut-outs for children who have difficulty finding things about themselves.

MATERIALS
- Magazines
- Scissors
- Glue
- Large poster board

Letter Special
(Ages 7 and up)

A fun and affirming exercise, Letter Special assists youngsters in realizing their special qualities. Group members get valuable practice in giving and receiving compliments. Most of all, this activity gives children permission to celebrate and own all of their unique gifts.

DESCRIPTION

With the children spread out comfortably on the floor the facilitator distributes paper and clipboards, then instructs youngsters to write their first names down the side of the paper with crayons, colored pencils, or markers. Group members may do so as creatively as possible, using special lettering (such as script, bubbled, or block) and different design and color combinations. The facilitator has extra paper on hand in case participants make a mistake or simply want to try something different. After everyone has finished, the facilitator collects the papers.

A brief discussion about special qualities follows as the group brainstorms a list of these traits, such as caring, honest, brave, smart, friendly, artistic, and gentle. The facilitator writes the group's thoughts on a greaseboard or newsprint. This valuable visual tool deeply enhances the quality of this experience.

Next the facilitator pulls out one paper from the pile and reads the name. Taking a moment to explain how people's names actually reflect some of their special gifts, the facilitator leads the group in brainstorming how each letter of the person's name represents one of his or her special gifts. For example, using Ben's name the group came up with bright, energetic, and nice. After Ben agreed to these gifts, the facilitator wrote each one horizontally on the page (see example). The process continues until each person's paper is filled with some of their special qualities. The activity concludes with a long and loud group cheer.

EXAMPLE

The group was hard at work when it came to Phil's turn. Within moments the qualities proud, happy, intelligent and loving were suggested. Phil accepted them all except proud, because he just didn't think it fit. For the next few minutes the group brainstormed to no avail, because Phil didn't think popular fit either. Finally the facilitator told Phil that it would be his task in the days ahead to find the right fit for P. Then the group celebrated the three qualities Phil had agreed upon. His smile almost filled the room.

AFFIRMATIONS

"Everyone has special qualities, including me."

"It's okay to feel good about myself."

"Today I will celebrate me."

COMMENTS

Take the time to brainstorm special qualities on the board.

The facilitator can play an active role in the brainstorming process by giving the group lots of solid ideas.

It's perfectly okay not to find a quality that fits every single letter in every person's name. Celebrate the letters of the person's name that you do come up with special gifts for, and let the child keep searching for gifts that correspond to the letters that remain.

MATERIALS

- Paper
- Clipboards
- Crayons
- Colored pencils
- Markers
- Greaseboard or newsprint

Example of
Letter Special

Polite

Helpful

Inteligent

Lively

I

Playful

The Car Wash
(Ages 7 and up)

An excellent follow-up to Affirmation Sensation, this activity deepens children's understanding and appreciation of affirmations. Youngsters gain valuable experience in giving and receiving affirmations in a fun and exciting way.

DESCRIPTION

Using affirmations that the group created in Affirmation Sensation, the facilitator directs the children to stand in two lines that face each other. Youngsters standing in the same line are approximately three feet apart, as are the two lines. In preparation, the facilitator makes sure the participants can all read their affirmation cards. The facilitator then instructs each child to hold his or her card in one hand. Youngsters raise their empty hands in the air and touch hands with the person across from them. This creates a tunnel effect similar to a car wash.

The facilitator demonstrates the activity by going first. Ducking slightly, the facilitator enters the car wash and stops at the first person to the right. That youngster reads his or her affirmation to the facilitator who pauses briefly to accept it and responds, "Thank-you." The facilitator repeats the process by turning to the person to the left. This activity continues until the facilitator goes through the entire car wash. Each youngster then goes through the car wash and is cleansed by a variety of affirmations. After everyone has had a chance to participate, a brief discussion ensues about the importance of self-care and affirmations.

EXAMPLE

Hal was often self-critical and harsh in group, as evidenced by the perpetual frown on his face. With some gentle coaxing from the other children he finally relented and went through the car wash. Amidst a variety of rich affirmations, a small grin appeared on his face. "Can I do that again right now?" he asked with a small giggle.

AFFIRMATIONS

"I can give and receive compliments."

COMMENTS

Because youngsters wrote two affirmation cards during the Affirmation Sensation, the facilitator may allow participants to rotate their cards throughout the exercise. The variety creates a richer experience and cuts down on possible boredom.

If there is an odd number of group members, the facilitator participates in the car wash to even things out. When this happens, the facilitator stands at the front of the line to help youngsters begin the process.

Once youngsters get the flow, the process moves fairly quickly. Youngsters can then go through the car wash two times in a row to reinforce the affirmations presented.

MATERIALS

• Affirmation cards from Affirmation Sensation

Inside Special
(Ages 7 and up)

This fun exercise reminds youngsters that their most special gifts are inside. It also deepens children's ability to give and receive affirmations.

DESCRIPTION

Prior to group the facilitator writes two simple yet different affirmations on small strips of paper for every member in group, folds the strips in half, and puts them inside uninflated balloons. Inside Special works well as a final follow-up exercise to Affirmation Sensation, Living Cards, I Am Special Bags, or Dressing For Dinner. After one of the above activities, the facilitator hands each child a balloon to blow up. Some youngsters may require assistance in inflating and tying their balloons.

After a brief follow-up discussion on celebrating special gifts, the facilitator instructs the children to pop their balloons with the pins provided and to explore the treasure within. Youngsters silently open the two affirmations and carefully read them. The facilitator then asks the members to put the affirmation that most suits them into their pockets and to give the other one to another person in the group. As youngsters give away the extra affirmation they get one in return from the person who received their affirmation. This process of giving and receiving may take up to three turns, at which point everyone keeps the affirmation in his or her possession. Children may share their affirmations with the group as the facilitator reviews how affirmations can help youngsters take good care of themselves.

EXAMPLE

After all the giving and receiving had taken place, a sly grin appeared on Joanne's face. When asked about her affirmations, this ten-year-old proudly declared, "I am capable" and "I am a beautiful child of God." When asked if those affirmations fit her she quickly responded, "Oh, yes!" and the grin turned into a huge smile.

AFFIRMATIONS

"I am lovable and capable."

"It's okay to feel good about myself."

"I can celebrate my special qualities."

COMMENTS

Be prepared to assist youngsters who have difficulty reading. Keeping the written affirmations basic and simple is helpful in this regard. The facilitator participates in this activity by positively modeling how to give and receive compliments in a healthy, balanced way.

MATERIALS

- Strips of paper with individual affirmations
- Balloons
- Pins

C H A P T E R   1 0

Friday

Celebrate Me — Good-byes and Hellos

KEY CONCEPTS
- I can leave my painful feelings and old ways behind. Good-bye to the old me.
- I can use the new skills and tools I've learned to take better care of myself. Hello to the new me.
- Today I celebrate talking, feeling, and trusting.

GOALS
- To let go of old cargo, painful feelings and self-defeating behaviors.
- To acknowledge new skills acquired during family week.
- To celebrate the newly learned skills and tools to take better care of oneself.
- To celebrate being a kid.

ACTIVITIES
Forgiveness and Reconciliation

Kids' Commencement

Kids' Commencement II

Children's Program Certificate

BOOKS/STORIES
The Happy Girl

What's So Special About Me? I'm One of a Kind

SONGS
"I Can Be The Best I Can Be" by Jim Newton (*Friends of the Family* cassette)

"Take a Step" by Peter Alsop (*In the Hospital* cassette)

"Take Me With You" by Peter Alsop (*Take Me With You* cassette)

"Friends of the Family" by Jim Newton (*Friends of the Family* cassette)

"Children At Heart" by Jim Newton (*Children At Heart* cassette)

DAILY THEME

Mini-Lecture

For many children growing up in addicted and/or codependent family systems, closure has largely been about abandonment and rejection. While youngsters protect themselves by putting up elaborate defenses, they deny themselves the opportunity to fully experience the wide array of feelings associated with time, events, and experiences coming to a close. Moreover, children also deny themselves the chance to fully celebrate their personhood and sense of connectedness to one another along the way. This can amount to another major loss for youngsters, one more missed opportunity to grow beyond those deep-seated and stifling messages of "it is my fault" and "I am alone."

Friday's focus is to celebrate all the miracles that have transpired during the week. Celebrate the incredible accomplishments, youngsters breaking the code of silence by preparing and delivering tough love lists, learning new problems solving and self-care strategies, beginning to own their special gifts, and simply enjoying their childhood through laughter and play. Celebrate all that the children are, precious, one-of-a-kind beings filled with joy, love, and goodness. Acknowledge and affirm their beauty and worth through celebration, as this gives youngsters a final boost as they head back home to life's many and varied challenges.

Closure is necessary in a variety of ways. Right up to and during the final phases of the forgiveness and reconciliation process, youngsters can fully let go of their old ways and painful feelings. In essence they are saying good-bye to the "old me", that part of the self engaged in behaviors that really didn't work. With this good-bye youngsters can say hello to the "new me", all those healthy skills they've acquired to take better care of themselves. Remind children not only what they've let go of during the week, but also acknowledge the new skills they've practiced and honed. Celebrate how their courage has led to talking, trusting, feeling, and finding the freedom to truly be a kid. While this theme permeates the day's activities, it is especially emphasized during the commencement proceedings, a rite of passage in the discovery and recovery process. These proceedings serve as a final moment of closure and celebration for the magic and miracles that have taken place during the week.

Celebrate!

Forgiveness and Reconciliation
(Ages 6 and up)

Youngsters complete the forgiveness and reconciliation process on Friday morning. This allows them to put the final touches on letting go of their old, self-defeating ways as they learn and practice new skills and tools to take better care of themselves. Such preparation serves to further enhance the day's theme of good-bye and hello, good-bye to the old ways and hello to the new ways of self-care and love.

DESCRIPTION

The facilitator leads the group in a brief discussion about forgiveness, particularly the importance of asking for it for one's self. Admitting one's mistakes and requesting forgiveness helps individuals to leave behind these transgressions and their resulting feelings. Once youngsters understand this concept, they begin to fill out forgiveness sheets for their family member in treatment. If youngsters get stumped in completing this task, the facilitator reminds them that they can use any information that had been listed by the patient or anything else for which they'd like forgiveness. The facilitator stresses this is a process, not an event, so youngsters don't get caught up in creating incredibly lengthy lists. They learn instead that this is another tool to use many times in the future to take better care of themselves. Roaming around the room as children work on their lists, the facilitator provides support, guidance, and encouragement.

For the reconciliation phase of this exercise most children prepare a card for the family member in treatment. Decorating the cards in a brightly colored, creative way, youngsters list all the things they like and love about that person. Occasionally children require assistance in putting into words exactly what these qualities are. The facilitator gives the group plenty of time to work on the cards, because they symbolize the deep love and caring the children have for these people.

MATERIALS

- Forgiveness Sheets
- Pencils
- Paper
- Crayons, colored pencils, and markers

Forgiveness List For _____(name)

Will you forgive me for:

Will you forgive me for:

Will you forgive me for:

Will you forgive me for:

Will you forgive me for:

Will you forgive me for:

Will you forgive me for:

Will you forgive me for:

Kids' Commencement
(For all ages)

While the family commencement exercises go far in acknowledging, affirming, and celebrating all the hard work done by family members throughout the week, they don't necessarily meet the youngsters' needs in a variety of ways. First, the children rarely graduate with all of their fellow group members because the commencement process is usually divided into two ceremonies. Second, the sheer size of family commencement intimidates many children and they are hesitant to share what this experience has been like for them in a room full of adults. To remedy this situation it is important for children to participate in their own commencement exercise prior to the family proceedings.

DESCRIPTION

Youngsters invite their parents and other family members to attend this brief ceremony. Family members watch as the children receive program certificates and listen as the youngsters speak about their experiences amidst their peers. Commencement proceedings conclude with parents and children in song, a symbol of hope in changing family legacies to ones of health and wellness. Children support and cheer for each other, providing hope for a beautiful today and a brighter tomorrow.

Kids' Commencement II
(For all ages)

Sometimes this optional activity is necessary to celebrate and affirm the incredible strides youngsters have made during the week. This occasion arises when patients and family members, due to assessments, doctor's appointments, or other special sessions, can't be present for the regular children's ceremonies.

DESCRIPTION

The facilitator leads this activity at either the beginning or end of the family commencement after making arrangements in advance with the family counselor who will be leading the proceedings. At the agreed upon time, the facilitator calls the children up to the stage for a special acknowledgment. He or she briefly describes the youngsters' hard work, courage, and willingness to learn throughout the week. For their efforts, each child will be awarded the illustrious Sierra Tucson STAR. The STAR, which stands for "starting totally awesome recovery," is a five-point golden star painted on the lid of a frozen juice container. A hole is punched at the top of the lid and a long piece of yarn is put through and tied in a knot so that the STAR can be worn like a gold medal. Each point on the STAR has a single letter, a reminder for the children of the different ways to take good care of themselves: *B* for Body, *M* for Mind, *F* for Feelings, and *S* for Spirit. The *K,* which is always at the top point of the STAR, represents the special importance of being a kid by taking the time to laugh and play. The facilitator acknowledges each youngster individually and puts the STAR around his or her neck. The audience claps and cheers after everyone has received the special award.

The advantage of this option is that the entire community can participate in these special proceedings.

MATERIALS

• Star Medals

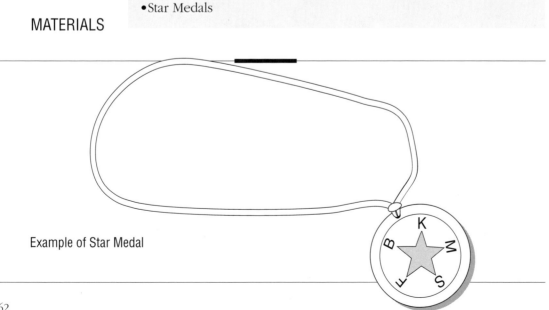

Example of Star Medal

Example of certificate

APPENDIX A: BOOKS

Brown, L.K. and Brown, M. *Dinosaurs Divorce – A Guide For Changing Families.* Boston, MA. Joy Street Books.

Crary, E. *I Can't Wait.* Seattle, WA. Parenting Press.

DiGiovanni, K. *My House Is Different.* Center City, MN. Hazelden.

Fosten-English, M. *Kids Are Special Curriculum.* San Jose, CA KAS.

Hastings, J., and Typpo, M. *An Elephant in the Living Room.* Minneapolis, MN. CompCare Publications.

Heide, F.P. and Worth-Van Clief, S. *That's What Friends Are For.* New York, NY. Scholastic Book Services.

Heyde, C. *The Happy Girl.* Marina Del Rey, CA. DeVorss and Company.

Jones, P. *The Brown Bottle.* Center City, MN. Hazelden.

McDonnell, J. and Ziegler, S. *What's So Special About Me? I'm One of a Kind.* Chicago, IL. Children's Press.

Melquist, E. *Pepper.* New York, NY. NCADD.

Millman, D. *Secret of the Peaceful Warrior.* Tiburon, CA. HJ Kramer Inc.

Moe, J., and Pohlman, D. *Kids' Power: Healing Games for Children of Alcoholics.* Deerfield Beach, FL. Health Communications.

Moe, J., and Ways, P. *Conducting Support Groups for Elementary School Children K-6: A Guide for Educators and Other Concerned Professionals.* Minneapolis, MN. Johnson Institute.

Palmer, Pat. *Liking Myself.* San Luis Obispo, CA. Impact Publishers.

Palmer, Pat. *The Mouse, the Monster, and Me.* San Luis Obispo, CA. Impact Publishers.

Patterson, S. *No-No, the Little Seal.* New York, NY. Random House.

Suerth, P. *I Would Prefer Not To.* Center City, MN. Hazelden.

APPENDIX B: FILMS

A Story About Feelings, Johnson Institute, 7205 Ohms Lane, Minneapolis, MN 55439-2159.

All Bottled Up, AIMS Media Inc., 626 Hustin Avenue, Glendale, CA 91201.

Francesca Baby, Walt Disney Educational Media Company, 500 South Buena Vista Street, Burbank, CA 91521.

Just Tipsy, Honey, ABC Afterschool Special, ABC, 2020 Avenue of the Stars, Fifth Floor, Century City, CA 90067.

Lots of Kids Like Us, Gerald T. Rodgers Productions, 5225 Old Orchard Road, Suite 23A, Skokie, IL 60077.

She Drinks a Little, Learning Corporation of America, 1350 Avenue of the Americas, New York, NY 10019.

The Cat Who Drank Too Much, FMS Productions, PO Box 4428, 520 E. Montecito Street, Suite F, Santa Barbara, CA 93140.

Twee, Fiddle, and Huff, Johnson Institute, 7205 Ohms Lane, Minneapolis, MN 55439-2159.

APPENDIX C: SONGS

Peter Alsop, Moose School Records, PO Box 960, Topanga, CA 90290, (310) 455-2318.

Jim Newton, Celebration Shop, PO Box 355, Bedford, TX 76021, (817) 268-0020.